Basic Macrobiotic Cooking

Procedures of Grain and Vegetable Cookery

by Julia Ferré

Edited by Laurel Ruggles

George Ohsawa Macrobiotic Foundation
Oroville, California

Illustrations by Jim North/Graphic Works
Back cover photograph by Chris Schneider

First edition 1987

©copyright 1987 by Julia Ferré, published by
George Ohsawa Macrobiotic Foundation
P.O. Box 426, Oroville, California 95965

Library of Congress Catalog Card Number: 86-83173
ISBN 0-918860-47-4

Foreword

I met Julia Ferre at the Moniteau Farm Summer Camp in central Missouri in 1980. She helped me with my cooking class, which was held in the poorly equipped farm barn. At such a class, she was a big help.

She came to our French Meadows Summer Camp in Northern California near Lake Tahoe a year later in much healthier condition. After the summer camp, she stayed with us at Vega Study Center as a kitchen helper. She remained and helped with my cooking classes for more than a year. Even with her busy schedule, she always found time for kindness to others, for example, baking many cookies and cakes for the Foundation staff at Christmas time.

I am very happy that her cookbook has finally materialized; this book is the first one written by one of my Vega students. This book is written by a busy, young mother who has continued to write during the time of just being married, establishing a new home, and while pregnant and nursing her first baby.

However, I am most happy with the publishing of this book because I am sure that this cookbook will be a great help to the many people who want to try this style of cooking, as well as those who have been practicing macrobiotics for some time, because it explains macrobiotic cooking thoroughly, clearly, and in easy-to-understand language.

I recommend her book highly to all macrobiotic followers, and especially for beginners.

Cornellia Aihara
November 1986

Preface

I'm an everyday cook, a wife and mother who prepares wholesome meals of grains and vegetables for my family – every day. I thoroughly enjoy cooking for my family and helping to keep each one healthy and happy. Although I serve fancy meals to guests and on special occasions, preparing simple yet satisfying meals on a daily basis gives me the most pleasure. I hope that you enjoy this same enthusiasm for the simple things in life.

The inspiration for this book resulted from a discussion in 1981 with Sandy Rothman, editor, and Carl Ferre (whom I would later marry), book manager of the George Ohsawa Macrobiotic Foundation. In considering the cookbooks that were available at that time, we concluded that there was a need for a cookbook which would explain the basics of macrobiotic cooking but would not require hard-to-find ingredients or time-consuming preparations or insist on a change to macrobiotic thinking. A book that could and would be used by more than those already committed to macrobiotics. A book that even my mother could use.

When I began macrobiotics in 1980, I had trouble using the available cookbooks. I was single, worked forty hours a week and often lacked the time or the energy to prepare elaborate dinners. I would page through the cookbooks for ideas, but would usually end up fixing boiled rice and steamed vegetables because they were easy and familiar. The cookbook I needed didn't exist. So when Sandy and Carl and I discussed cookbooks, I immediately thought of writing the macrobiotic cookbook I had needed as a beginner. The book would emphasize the cooking one does on a daily basis and the procedures one needs to cook good quality meals every day.

Since I was working with Cornellia Aihara at the Vega Study

Center, I was in the fortunate position of learning from a cooking master. For over a year, I assisted Cornellia in daily cooking classes and observed how she balanced meals, planned menus, and changed the cooking with the seasons. As I learned about many new foods and techniques, I began to keep a diary, grouping together dishes which were similar in technique in order to organize my writing on procedures.

When Carl and I moved to Texas in 1982, I then had the opportunity to practice daily macrobiotic cooking on my own. I had the challenge of following the basic principles I had learned from Cornellia at Vega but under new and changing circumstances. The climate was very different, I was again working forty hours a week, and then I had a baby. The cookbook started taking form as I drew from these experiences.

Many people have contributed to this book by helping me both directly and indirectly. I wish to express my deepest appreciation to George and Lima Ohsawa, who originally spread macrobiotic thought and cooking techniques throughout the world and have led so many people to happier and healthier lives; to Herman and Cornellia Aihara, my teachers, who have shared macrobiotics with me and many others in a personal and practical way; and to Cornellia for many helpful suggestions, and for writing the preface.

My sincere thanks to my parents, John and Diana Karlen, and to Carl's parents, Gustave and Dorothy Ferre, for their loving advice and support; and to my husband, Carl, for inspiring and helping me to write, for testing the recipes, and for his continual guidance; and to our sons Gus and Nels for being a part of our family and for the immediate reactions on their faces which teach me so much.

I also wish to thank Sandy Rothman for the original inspiration and for reading the manuscript and adding numerous suggestions; Laurel Ruggles for her precise editing work to help me write what I'm really trying to say; and to the George Ohsawa Macrobiotic Foundation and staff for all their work in publishing this book.

Julia Ferre
November 1986

Contents

Fish and Eggs   97

Salads and Dressings   105

Sauces and Condiments   119

Introduction

Once you know how to scramble eggs, you can scramble eggs, whether you have four eggs or twelve, have a different pan, or are camping. So it is with macrobiotic cooking. Once you know how to pressure cook brown rice, make soup, or prepare hijiki, you can cook these items, whether the measures are varied, vegetables are small or large, or the utensils or stove are different.

This book is about basic grain and vegetable cookery, with an emphasis on the how-to's of cooking. There are good recipes too, of course, but to me, cooking is more than just so much of this with so much of that sauteed for so much time. Cooking is an integration of ingredients and technique. And macrobiotic cooking has a third element, a principle which helps you create order in and through your cooking. This book will give you an introduction to macrobiotic cooking – the foods, the procedures, and the principles.

Learning macrobiotic cooking – You can delve right in and start learning about macrobiotic foods, cooking methods, and principles all at once, or you can take your time and learn at a slower pace. At the very beginning, start by cooking foods you know you will eat and use techniques with which you are comfortable. Include new, unfamiliar foods and new, unfamiliar procedures as you are ready, perhaps one new food or procedure per meal; if it doesn't turn out, you still have a meal. If you are using a new procedure, use familiar foods at first. If you wish to prepare a new food, then use a familiar procedure. In this manner you change gradually and can avoid overwhelming yourself with many new foods and procedures at once. Thus, you can assimilate the ideas and remember them better.

1

Your first meal – If you have just picked up this book and want to prepare dinner right now, go to the large section of sample menus on pages 211 to 223. The "Beginning Menus" are basic, using easily found foods and simple techniques. Later, come back here and read the rest of this chapter.

Making the transition – Adopting a macrobiotic approach to daily diet is a big change for most people, because many of the foods and cooking techniques are new, and there is much cooking involved. As you change, keep in mind that the refined and processed foods are replaced with wholesome, whole foods. Try to eliminate preservatives, dyes, and artificial ingredients completely. In addition, replace:

red meat with fowl, fish, and grains and beans in combination.

refined sugars with fresh fruit and natural sweeteners.

refined grains and grain products with whole grains and grain products.

canned and frozen vegetables with fresh vegetables.

heavily sugared or salted snacks with good quality snacks of wholesome ingredients.

You can make the change in two weeks or two years depending on your own preference. A gentle transition may be easier for you, your family, and friends to assimilate and accept. On the other hand your present condition may make a faster change more desirable.

How To Use This Book

How recipes are arranged – This book is organized by procedures rather than by recipes and thus the procedure itself is listed first. Sample recipes used with that procedure are listed second. Comments are listed third, covering information about that particular procedure, variations, and ideas for more recipes.

You may wish to consult the index to find recipes for a specific item such as brown rice or winter squash. Or, you may prefer to page through the grain section until you reach a brown rice recipe you want to use. Either way, make sure to read the first page of that section, which contains general information. Then read through the entire procedure.

Measurements – Setting out the measurements was the most difficult part of writing this book. What is standard? Many factors affect how the dish will turn out. For example, I may use 2 cups of rolled oats with 5 cups of water to prepare oatmeal, yet the consistency will vary if I use a different pot or a different brand of oats, or if I am cooking in summer or winter. I may want a softer or harder oatmeal if I'm sick or if it has been very cold and so I use slightly different measurements.

The listed amounts in the recipes are ones I generally use for a moderate situation of climate and health. They are neither overly yin nor yang for me, living in Northern California. If you live in a very hot or very cold climate or have specific dietary needs, you may need to adjust the amounts.

A very important macrobiotic principle to learn is the one of change. Life's many facets constantly change and our cooking needs change also. Therefore when using measurements from this book, use them as guidelines to help you become familiar with the ingredients, the procedures, and the desired flavor of the resulting dish. And when you are ready, change the recipe and use your own measurements, exact or intuitive.

Adapting and adjusting recipes – All the recipes can be enlarged. Most can be reduced, too. One way to adjust recipes is to use the same proportion, halving or doubling every ingredient. Another way is to change the proportions. Use two onions instead of one with the same amounts of the remaining ingredients. When changing the proportions, maintain the same consistency to produce the desired end product. For example, if you have slightly more noodles than the recipe calls for and you wish to add them, add more water.

Recipes can be adapted by substituting ingredients. The focus of this book is on procedures and not on ingredients. Use procedures with similar foods to make new recipes. Try almond butter in place of sesame butter, collards rather than kale, or red beans in place of pinto beans. You can create many dishes by following the basic procedures and substituting ingredients.

Estimating numbers of servings – It is difficult to spell out exact quantities in terms of numbers of servings because serving sizes and appetites vary. The recipes in the book have no set numbers of servings; only an approximate yield in terms of cups, number of muffins, etc. The yield will vary depending on your measuring, the size of the vegetables, and the temperature of the stove. Variations from ½ cup to 1 cup of water, a small bunch to a medium bunch, or medium-low heat to low heat can affect the yield. So yields and numbers of servings are always approximate.

The list of suggested serving amounts on page 228 may help you to estimate how many servings a certain yield will give you. Then you can determine if you need to change the quantities in the recipe. You also can jot down your experience with each recipe regarding serving size.

Critiquing this book – The book is meant to be useful; therefore, follow through with the recipes. After trying a recipe, critique it. Did you have success? Did you really like the combination? Or burn the pot? Use the white spaces in the book to write your own comments and questions. If the text covers a point you feel is very strong, or a point which is unclear, make a note of it. Perhaps your question will be answered elsewhere in this book, perhaps in other books, or perhaps you will answer it from your own experience.

No matter how much you study and practice cooking, there is always more to discover. I hope this book will help you in your cooking and will inspire you to learn more about macrobiotics.

Grains

Washing – Grain is washed to remove the dust that settles on it when it is husked to remove the outer shell. To clean, measure the full quantity of grain to be used into a cooking pan. Add water, swirl, and drain. Repeat 2 times. If the rinse water is still cloudy, repeat until the water is clear. Buckwheat, flaked grains, pastas, and creamed cereals don't require washing.

Soaking – Soaking whole grain before cooking allows the grain to swell. The kernels become soft and cook faster than if unsoaked. The cooked grain will taste sweeter. The soaking time can vary depending on the grain, the time of year, the location, and your own schedule. Hard-kernelled grains such as whole oats, wheat, rye, and barley cook better when soaked first, from 4 to 8 hours. Rice can be soaked if desired, from 1 to 8 hours. Millet and buckwheat do not require soaking because they have thinner kernel walls and cook quickly. You can soak grains at any season of the year. Generally, when it is hot, soak for a shorter time than when it is cold. If there is no time for soaking, grain can be cooked by using more water and a longer cooking time. When cooked, unsoaked grains will be more chewy and less sticky than soaked grains.

Salt – The addition of salt in cooking helps to break down the grain, and the grain is sweeter to the taste. Also, salt is alkaline-forming and balances the acid-forming grains. If grains are to be soaked, add salt after soaking, just before cooking.

5

Cooking times – Generally, hard-kernelled grains need to be cooked longer than soft-kernelled grains or grains which are cut, rolled, or creamed. Within the times specified, the longer cooking times produce a more soft and creamy grain.

> *Brown rice, whole wheat, whole rye, whole oats, whole and pearled barley* – 45 minutes to 2 hours. These hard-kernelled grains are often soaked before cooking.

> *Buckwheat, millet, cracked wheat, bulghur, steel-cut oats, flaked (rolled) grains, cornmeal, and creamed cereals* – 30 minutes to 1 hour.

> *Couscous and pastas* – 5 to 15 minutes.

Heat – Use medium to medium-high heat to bring grain to full pressure or to a boil. Then reduce heat as directed. For longer cooking times, use a flame tamer under the pot to prevent burning.

Lifting cover and stirring – Let grain cook; do not lift the cover or stir while it is cooking. If the cover is removed and the grain is stirred, steam escapes which causes heat loss, and the grain will not cook completely. Grain sticking to the bottom of the pan is not a problem; after cooking, let stand 5 to 10 minutes before removing the cover and mixing. The steam will lift the bottom grain from the pan so it can be mixed with the rest of the grain.

Mixing – After grain is cooked and allowed to stand 5 to 10 minutes, mix with a dampened wooden spoon or rice paddle. Slip spoon between grain and the side of the pan, going all around the pan. Gently but thoroughly mix grains from top to bottom.

Cleaning the utensils – Soak cookware, utensils, and bowls in cold water 5 to 10 minutes to remove any sticking kernels. Then wash in hot water.

Pressure Cooked Grain

Procedure – Wash grain. Soak if desired or directed in the full quantity of water. Add salt after soaking. Lock cover on pot. Place weight on cover. Place cooker over medium-high heat. Bring to full pressure (15 pounds). Slip a flame tamer under the cooker and turn heat to low. Cook at full pressure for the time indicated. See page 239 for further information on using a pressure cooker.

Short or long grain brown rice – Soak 1 to 8 hours. Pressure cook 45 minutes. Yield: 5 to 6 cups.

> 4 cups brown rice
> 4 to 5 cups water
> ¼ tsp. salt

Barley, whole oats, whole wheat, or whole rye – Soak 4 to 8 hours. Pressure cook 45 minutes. Yield: 5 to 6 cups.

> 4 cups grain
> 6 cups water
> ¼ tsp. salt

Brown rice combinations – For the second ingredient, use long grain brown or wild rice, whole oats, whole rye, whole wheat, barley, or millet. Soak 1 to 8 hours. Pressure cook 45 minutes. Yield: 8 to 9 cups.

> 4 cups short grain brown rice
> 1 cup other grain
> 7 cups water
> ¼ tsp. salt

Brown rice and bean combinations – Use azuki beans, mung beans, kidney beans, or chickpeas. Soak 4 to 8 hours. Pressure cook 45 minutes. Yield: 7 to 8 cups.

---

4 cups brown rice
½ cup beans
6 to 7 cups water
¼ tsp. salt

Whole oats and rye – Soak 6 to 8 hours. Pressure cook 45 minutes to 1 hour. Yield: 6 to 7 cups.

---

3 cups whole oats
1 cup whole rye
6 cups water
¼ tsp. salt

Whole wheat and barley – Soak 6 to 8 hours. Pressure cook 45 minutes to 1 hour. Yield: 6 to 7 cups.

---

2 cups whole wheat
2 cups barley
6 cups water
¼ tsp. salt

Millet – Millet does not need to be soaked, but does require more water than the standard proportion. Pressure cook 20 minutes. Yield: 8 to 9 cups.

---

4 cups millet
8 cups water
¼ tsp. salt

Rice Porridge – Soak 1 to 8 hours. Pressure cook 1 to 1½ hours. Yield: 6 to 7 cups.

---

2 cups brown rice
6 cups water
¼ tsp. salt

Comments – Pressure cooking is a quick and thorough way to cook whole grains which have a hard kernel. It is generally not called for when cooking buckwheat, or grains which are cut, flaked, or creamed. Most grains pressure cook better when soaked first. Rice, wheat, and rye may be cooked without soaking, but are more chewy. If unsoaked, use ½ cup more water and pressure cook 15 minutes longer. Always soak barley and whole oats because they may clog the pressure cooker vent if not soaked.

The amount of water, grain, and salt varies with the size and condition of the pressure cooker and the quantity of grain being cooked. In a 4 to 6 quart pressure cooker, cook at least 4 cups grain; smaller amounts do not cook well. If you wish to cook less, use a tiny pressure cooker, such as a 2 quart or 1.8 liter size. Another way is to use a bowl inside the pressure cooker: Place 2 cups grain soaked in 3 cups water in a pyrex or stainless steel bowl with ⅛ teaspoon salt. Place 2 cups water in the bottom of the cooker. Fit the bowl into the cooker. Pressure cook as in the standard procedure.

When cooking 4 or more cups of grain, use a standard proportion of 1 cup grain to 1¼ cups water for rice. For other hard-kernelled grains (wheat, rye, barley, and whole oats) used alone or in combination, use equal amounts of grain and water plus 2 more cups of water (4 grain and 6 water; 5 grain and 7 water). If you want softer grain, add more water. When pressure cooking grain which has not been soaked, use the given proportions and add an extra ½ cup of water. Use ¼ teaspoon salt for 4 cups grain.

When cooking, a certain amount of water changes to steam and evaporates. A new pressure cooker has a very tight seal and less water evaporates than with an older pressure cooker. You can use 1 cup water per 1 cup grain in a new cooker. Remember to cook at least 4 cups grain in a large pressure cooker; 1 cup rice and 1 cup water will burn.

Boiled Grain, Soaked

Procedure – Wash and drain grain. Soak for the desired time in the full quantity of water. Add salt after soaking. Cover. Bring to a boil. Simmer over low heat for the time indicated, using a flame tamer if needed.

Brown rice – Soak 1 to 8 hours. Simmer 1 to 1½ hours. Yield: 8 to 10 cups.

> 4 cups brown rice
> 8 cups water
> ¼ tsp. salt

Barley, whole oats, whole wheat, or whole rye – Soak 4 to 8 hours. Simmer 1½ to 2 hours. Yield: 8 cups.

> 3 cups grain
> 6 cups water
> scant ¼ tsp. salt

Porridge – Simmer for the time listed above for specific grain. Yield: 4 or more cups.

> 1 cup grain
> 4 cups water, or more
> pinch salt

Comments – Soaking grains before boiling works well for those grains that have a hard kernel. If unable to soak, use ½ to 1 cup more water and simmer 30 minutes longer. For variety, mix grains in the basic proportion of 2 cups water to 1 cup grain and simmer for 1½ to 2 hours.

Boiled Grain, Unsoaked, Hot Water

Procedure – Bring water to a boil. Add salt, then grain. Cover. Bring to a boil. Simmer over low heat for the time indicated, using a flame tamer if needed.

Millet – Wash and drain before cooking. Simmer 30 minutes. Yield: 6 to 7 cups.

> 2 cups millet
> 6 cups water
> ⅛ tsp. salt

Couscous – Bring to a rolling boil, which will cause the couscous to foam. Remove from heat and let stand 5 to 10 minutes before serving. Yield: 2 to 3 cups.

> 2 cups couscous
> 2 to 2½ cups water
> ⅛ tsp. salt

Comments – Boiling grain in cold water and boiling grain in hot water are similar procedures; they use the same grains, cooking times, and number of utensils. However, the grains cook differently. In the cold water method, everything is mixed together first, and the grain tends to swell more as it comes to a boil. In the hot water method, the grain is added to the water and tends to swell only slightly because it is immediately surrounded by hot water. The flavors are subtly different.

Boiled Grain, Unsoaked, Cold Water

Procedure – Place grain, cold water, and salt in a pan. Cover. Bring to a boil. Simmer over low heat for the time indicated, using a flame tamer if needed.

Buckwheat (purchased roasted) – Simmer 30 minutes. Yield: 4 to 5 cups.

> 2 cups buckwheat
> 3¾ to 4 cups water
> ⅛ tsp. salt

Oatmeal or other flaked grains – Simmer 30 minutes. Yield: 4 to 6 cups.

> 2 cups grain
> 4 to 5 cups water
> ⅛ tsp. salt

Cracked wheat or steel-cut oats – Simmer 45 minutes to 1 hour. Yield: 4 to 5 cups.

> 2 cups grain
> 4 cups water
> ⅛ tsp. salt

Bulghur, cornmeal, or creamed cereals – Use a wire whisk to mix cornmeal and creamed cereals with water to prevent lumping. Simmer 30 minutes. Yield: 4 to 6 cups.

> 2 cups grain
> 4 to 5 cups water
> ⅛ tsp. salt

Comments – Boiling is the method used for unsoaked whole grains with a thin kernel wall and for grains that are rolled or cut. Cornmeal and creamed grains, coarsely ground flour cooked into porridge such as rice cream or wheat cream, cook well by this method but are more flavorful when roasted first, see page 14. Some grains, especially oatmeal, tend to boil over, so leave the cover slightly ajar. Roasted grains are less likely to boil over.

For variety, try mixing grains and flakes. Use the basic proportions and times listed for specific grains. Try oatmeal with buckwheat or rye flakes; or millet with steel-cut oats. Another variation is to add onion to the grain: Mince 1 small onion and mix with either millet or bulghur so they simmer together. Or, add minced scallions: Place scallions on top of buckwheat or cornmeal during the last 2 minutes of cooking.

Boiled Grain, Roasted

Procedure – Heat water. Place grain in dry pan (no oil) and dry roast over medium heat for 2 to 10 minutes, stirring constantly. (Washed grains require a longer time because they dry first before roasting.) Roast grain until fragrant and lightly browned; whole grains will pop.

Mix roasted grain, boiling water, and salt in a pan. Cover. Bring to a boil. Simmer over low heat for the time indicated, using a flame tamer if needed.

Brown rice – Wash and drain before roasting. Simmer 1 hour. Yield: 9 to 10 cups.

4 cups brown rice
8 cups water
¼ tsp. salt

Buckwheat (purchased raw) – Simmer 30 minutes. Yield: 4 to 5 cups.

2 cups buckwheat
4 cups water
⅛ tsp. salt

Millet – Wash and drain before roasting. Simmer 30 minutes. Yield: 6 to 7 cups.

2 cups millet
6 cups water
⅛ tsp. salt

Oatmeal, cornmeal, creamed cereals, or other rolled or cut grains – Use a wire whisk to mix cornmeal and creamed cereals with water to prevent lumping. Simmer 30 minutes. Yield: 4 to 5 cups.

2 cups grain
4 to 5 cups water
⅛ tsp. salt

Comments – Preparing roasted, boiled grain requires two utensils and can be done in two ways depending on utensils. One way is to add water to grain; the other is to add grain to water. I like to roast in cast iron ware and prepare various grains differently. For example, I roast cornmeal and buckwheat in a Dutch oven and add boiling water to them, and I roast rice in a skillet and add it to boiling water.

Roasting the grain before boiling makes the dish more flavorful. Buckwheat, cornmeal, and creamed cereals are especially good when roasted, but all grains may be roasted for added flavor. For a variation, add minced onion and simmer with the grain. Or, add minced scallions to grain during the last 2 minutes of cooking, by placing on top of grain and steaming.

Boiled Grain, Sauteed

Procedure – Heat water in a kettle. Heat oil in a pan and add grain. Saute until fragrant, stirring constantly. Add boiling water and salt. Cover. Bring to a boil. Simmer 30 minutes over low heat, using a flame tamer if needed.

Cornmeal, buckwheat, or bulghur – Yield: 4 to 5 cups.

4 cups water
1 tsp. corn oil
2 cups cornmeal, buckwheat, or bulghur
¼ tsp. salt

Millet – Yield: 6 to 7 cups.

6 cups water
1 tsp. corn oil
2 cups millet
¼ tsp. salt

Comments – Sauteing grain in oil produces a very flavorful grain dish. Any grain may be sauteed, but cornmeal, bulghur, millet, and buckwheat are especially good.

Boiled Grain with Sauteed Vegetables

Procedure - Heat water in a kettle. Heat oil in a pan and add vegetables, one kind at a time, in the order listed. Saute each kind briefly. Add grain. Saute until fragrant, stirring constantly. Add boiling water and salt. Cover. Bring to a boil. Simmer 30 minutes over low heat, using a flame tamer if needed.

Grain with onion - Yield: 4 to 5 cups (millet: 6 to 7 cups).

1 tsp. corn oil
1 medium onion, minced
2 cups grain (bulghur, cornmeal, millet, etc.)
¼ tsp. salt
4 cups water (for millet, add 2 cups additional water)

Cornmeal with green pepper - Yield: 5 to 6 cups.

1 tsp. corn oil
1 medium onion, minced
1 medium green bell pepper, diced
2 cups cornmeal
4 cups water
¼ tsp. salt

Bulghur with mushrooms - Yield: 5 to 6 cups.

1 tsp. corn oil
1 medium onion, minced
12 medium mushrooms, diced
2 cups bulghur
4 cups water
¼ tsp. salt

Comments - Grain boiled with sauteed vegetables is a flavorful dish which makes a nice meal with beans or a sauce. Try millet with onion, celery, and carrot, or buckwheat with onion and celery.

Boiled Grain, Layered with Vegetables

Procedure – Heat water in a kettle. Heat oil in a pan and add vegetables, one kind at a time, in the order listed. Saute each kind briefly. Add ¼ cup water. Layer grain over vegetables. Cover. Steam 5 minutes. Add remainder of boiling water without disturbing layers. Add salt. Cover. Bring to a boil. Simmer 30 minutes over low heat.

Millet with vegetables – Yield: 7 to 8 cups.

1 tsp. corn oil
1 medium onion, minced
2 medium stalks celery, diced
1 small carrot, thin quarter rounds
2 cups millet, washed and drained
6 cups water
¼ tsp. salt

Comments – Layering grain over sauteed vegetables produces a light and fluffy dish. The grain won't stick to the pan because the vegetables are on the bottom. Try other grain and vegetable combinations, such as millet or cornmeal layered over onions and winter squash, or bulghur layered over zucchini or bell peppers.

Baked Grain

Procedure – Heat water. Wash and drain grain, if necessary. Roast grain in a dry skillet (no oil) until fragrant, stirring constantly, about 5 minutes. Place roasted grain, salt, and boiling water in a casserole dish. Cover. Bake for the time indicated at 350 degrees.

> **Brown rice –** Wash and drain before roasting. Bake 1 hour. Yield: 6 to 7 cups.
>
> ---
>
> 3 cups brown rice
> 6 cups water
> ⅛ tsp. salt
>
> ---

> **Millet –** Wash and drain before roasting. Bake 30 minutes. Yield: 6 to 7 cups.
>
> ---
>
> 2 cups millet
> 6 cups water
> ⅛ tsp. salt
>
> ---

Comments – Baking roasted grain produces a pilaf-type dish, which goes well with holiday menus. Try baking roasted bulghur or adding sauteed vegetables to bake with the grain, topping with roasted sunflower or pumpkin seeds.

Rice Balls

Procedure – Cut one sheet of nori into 12 squares. Dampen hands. Press cooked rice into a ball. Make a hole in the center. Place umeboshi plum in the hole. Press again to close hole. Cover ball with 2 pieces of nori, partially covering the rice ball.

Rice ball

¼ to ½ cups cooked brown rice
½ small umeboshi plum
2 pieces cut nori

Comments – Rice balls are best when rice is fresh. Use warm pressure cooked rice as it is easy to form into balls. Let cool before placing nori on rice balls as hot rice will cook and crinkle the nori. Rice balls are good for traveling. The umeboshi in the center helps to keep them fresh longer. For variety, use a mixed rice, such as brown rice with azuki beans, or use roasted, chopped sunflower seeds or sesame salt to cover the rice balls.

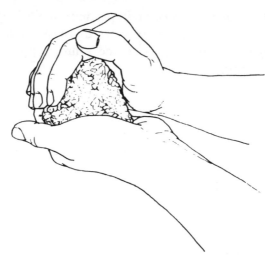

Noodles

Preparations – There are two basic ways to prepare noodles. Noodles can be cooked and drained, and then served or mixed with other ingredients. Or, noodles can be cooked together with the other ingredients. Noodles cooked separately can be used in salads, casseroles, or served in broth, and are great for kids, who often like noodles just as they are. Cooking noodles together with the other ingredients saves time, uses fewer utensils, and makes a creamy soup or a one-pot meal. For recipes that have noodles cooked into them, see soups and beans sections.

Noodles and salt – Japanese noodles such as udon (wheat) and soba (buckwheat) sometimes contain salt while American pastas usually do not. Check the package. If salted, boil in unsalted water. If unsalted, boil in salted water. When cooking noodles into dishes, add less salt when using noodles that have salt in them.

Cooking time – Noodles require 10 to 15 minutes to boil and become soft. They are done when they are tender and have the same color throughout. When cooking noodles separately, they should be cooked until tender, but still firm. If too soft, they may fall apart when serving or mixing into the dish. When cooking noodles into a dish, add during the last 15 to 20 minutes of cooking the dish and cook until tender and soft, so they will almost melt in your mouth.

Serving – Cooked noodles can be served with broths, soups, sauces, or garnishes. Since the noodles will absorb the flavor, more than the usual amount of seasoning will be required. Cooked noodles also can be used in salads, sea vegetable dishes, and casseroles.

To make the serving of long spaghetti noodles easier, don't just dump all the noodles into the bowl. Instead, place noodles into the bowl by the handful with a twisting motion. Then, when serving, it is easy to pick up one serving at a time without pulling out all the noodles.

Boiled Noodles, Shock Method

Procedure – Bring water to a boil over medium heat. Add salt if needed. Add noodles and stir to separate them. Cover pan. Bring to a rolling boil. Add ½ cup cold water and stir noodles. Bring to a rolling boil again. Add ½ cup cold water and stir noodles. Bring to a rolling boil a third time. Add ½ cup cold water and stir noodles. Bring to a rolling boil again. Remove from heat and let stand 2 to 3 minutes. Noodles are done when they are the same color inside and out. Drain. Rinse in cold water. Drain. Rinse and drain again, if needed, until noodles are cooled.

Noodles – Yield: 4 to 5 cups per 8 oz. noodles.

10 to 12 cups water for up to 16 oz. of noodles (16 oz. of noodles will absorb 8 cups of water completely)
¼ tsp. salt for 10 to 12 cups water (if noodles are unsalted)

Comments – This method of shocking noodles involves bringing the noodles to a rolling boil (noodles almost foam out of the pan), and adding cold water three times. The cold water temporarily halts the cooking of the outside of the noodle so the inside of the noodle can become soft without overcooking the outside. Noodles cooked by shocking will be cooked uniformly throughout.

The cooking and rinse waters can be saved for later use. Cool to room temperature and refrigerate. Use within 2 to 3 days to cook other grains, soups, crackers, and breads.

Boiled Noodles, Soak Method

Procedure – Bring water to a boil over medium heat. Add salt if needed. Add noodles and stir to separate them. Cover pan. Bring to a rolling boil. Add ½ cup cold water and stir noodles. Bring to a rolling boil again. Remove from heat. Let noodles soak in the hot water 15 to 20 minutes, covered, until tender (noodles should be the same color inside and out). Drain. Rinse in cold water and drain. Repeat if needed until noodles are cool.

Noodles – Yield: 4 to 5 cups per 8 oz. noodles.

10 to 12 cups water for up to 16 oz. of noodles (16 oz. of noodles will absorb 8 cups of water completely)
¼ tsp. salt for 10 to 12 cups water (if noodles are unsalted)

Comments – This method of soaking noodles involves bringing the noodles to a rolling boil (noodles almost foam out of the pan) and adding cold water once to shock. Soaking noodles in the hot water saves energy. This method also produces noodles which are uniformly cooked throughout. However, don't oversoak as they can become mushy.

Vegetables

Using the whole vegetable – Try to use as much of the vegetable as possible, including the skin. Most vegetable skins are edible, and even the skin of winter squash is tender when cooked. Cabbage hearts and broccoli stems are delicious, too. Any woody parts can be trimmed.

Cleaning – Clean vegetables to remove bad spots and dirt. Peel onions and waxed vegetables. Sort through greens to remove bugs and wilted or discolored leaves. Some roots have embedded dirt. Use the inside point of the knife to scrape off this dirt as shown in the illustration.

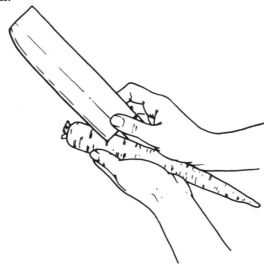

Washing – After cleaning, wash. Scrub roots well with a vegetable brush. Immerse leafy greens and scallions individually in a basin of water to clean thoroughly. Don't take short cuts when washing vegetables. It may seem faster just to rinse under the faucet, but it doesn't remove all the dirt.

Cutting – Learn and use different cutting styles. When different vegetables are cooked together, use different cuts so the dish is more attractive. However, cut vegetables in similar sizes so the dish will cook evenly. Generally, when vegetables are young and tender, cuts can be larger than when vegetables are old and tougher. Also, when vegetables are cooked alone, cuts can be larger than when vegetables are cooked in combination. For cutting styles, see pages 247–257.

Cooking and timing – Overcooking can ruin some vegetables (broccoli becomes mushy), while undercooking can ruin others (butternut squash remains hard). Generally, green vegetables can be slightly undercooked, and orange/yellow vegetables can be slightly overcooked. The age of the vegetable affects the length of cooking. Younger vegetables are more tender than older vegetables and require shorter cooking times. Cuts, too, affect the length of cooking. Smaller pieces cook faster than larger pieces.

Other Cooking methods – Procedures for boiling vegetables can be found under Cooked Salads, pages 106–109, and under Stews, page 48.

Baked Vegetables, Whole

Procedure – Prick vegetables with fork, knife, or ice pick so that there are air holes on top, every inch or so. Place vegetables on a flat baking sheet. Bake 1 to 1½ hours at 350 degrees until vegetables are soft and a fork can be inserted easily.

Baked vegetables – Use any combination, singly or mixed, of the following.

butternut or acorn winter squash, small to medium
sweet potatoes, medium to large
potatoes, large
turnips, medium
onions, large

Comments – It is easy to bake whole vegetables; however, not all vegetables can be baked. This method works best with vegetables that retain their shape such as root vegetables. To make the skin softer, lightly oil the vegetables before baking.

Baked Vegetables, Cut

Procedure – Mix vegetables, salt, and water in a casserole dish. Cover. Bake 45 minutes to 1 hour at 350 degrees.

Winter squash – Yield: 3 to 4 cups.

2 to 3 lbs. winter squash, 1½-inch squares
⅛ tsp. salt
¼ cup water

Carrots and onion – Yield: 4 to 5 cups.

1 medium onion, minced
4 medium carrots, diced or shaved
¼ tsp. salt
¼ cup water

Sweet potatoes and parsnips – Yield: 5 to 6 cups.

1 medium onion, thick crescents
3 medium sweet potatoes, logs
2 medium parsnips, large matchsticks
¼ tsp. salt
½ cup water

Comments – Baking cut vegetables with water brings out their sweetness. Vegetables become softer than if they are baked whole. Also, baking with water allows you to bake vegetables which can not be baked whole. Try baking leeks and other kinds of squash, too.

Layered Vegetables

Procedure – Heat oil in a pan. Saute onion until transparent. Add water. Layer vegetables in the order listed. Sprinkle salt on top. Cover. Bring to a boil. Simmer 25 to 30 minutes over low heat.

Cabbage and carrots – Yield: 5 to 6 cups.

½ tsp. sesame oil
1 medium onion, thin crescents
1 medium cabbage;
   core, diced
   leaves, 1-inch squares
1 large carrot, large matchsticks
½ cup water
¼ tsp. salt

Winter squash and carrots – Yield: 6 to 7 cups.

½ tsp. sesame oil
1 medium onion, thin crescents
½ cup water
1 medium butternut squash, 2-inch squares
3 medium carrots, small chunks
¼ tsp. salt

Summer squash and green beans – Yield: 6 to 7 cups.

½ tsp. sesame oil
1 medium onion, thin crescents
½ cup water
4 medium yellow squash, paper cut
20 medium green beans, 3-inch lengths
¼ tsp. salt

Brussels sprouts, cauliflower, and carrots – Yield: 10 to 12 cups.

½ tsp. sesame oil
1 medium onion, thin crescents
½ cup water
½ medium cauliflower, large flowerettes
12 medium Brussels sprouts, whole
4 medium carrots, large chunks
½ tsp. salt

Comments – Layering is a simple way to cook 3 or 4 kinds of vegetables together. Onion is sauteed first to add flavor. Then the vegetables are layered from yin at the bottom to yang on the top. There are many possible combinations. Try using greens, leeks, shaved corn, or uncommon vegetables such as sunchokes.

Layered Vegetables with Cornmeal

Procedure – Roast cornmeal in a dry pan until fragrant, 2 to 3 minutes, stirring constantly. Remove and set aside. Using the same pan, heat oil. Saute onion until transparent. Add water. Layer vegetables in the order listed. Sprinkle cornmeal on top. Sprinkle salt on top of the cornmeal. Cover. Bring to a boil. Simmer 30 minutes over low heat. Mix, cover, and let stand 5 minutes before serving. Cornmeal will absorb all the liquid.

Collard greens with cornmeal – Yield: 6 to 7 cups.

½ cup fine cornmeal
1 tsp. sesame oil
1 medium onion, thin crescents
1½ cups water
1 medium bunch collard greens;
    stems, thin rounds
    leaves, shredded
¼ tsp.salt

Green peppers with cornmeal – Yield: 5 to 6 cups.

½ cup fine cornmeal
1 tsp. sesame oil
1 medium onion, thin crescents
1½ cups water
4 medium green bell peppers, thin crescents
¼ tsp. salt

Comments – Layering with cornmeal produces a hearty vegetable dish which is nice in the winter. It is a delicious way to serve greens. Try other vegetables in combination, layering from yin to yang, such as onion, cabbage, turnip, and carrot.

Pressure Cooked Vegetables

Procedure – Place vegetables, water, and salt in a pressure cooker. Bring to full pressure (15 lbs.). Cook for the time indicated. Bring pressure down immediately by running cold water over the cooker.

Butternut squash and onions – Pressure cook 8 to 10 minutes. Yield: 6 cups.

3 large onions, halved
1 large butternut squash, 3-inch squares
½ cup water
¼ tsp. salt

Turnips, rutabagas, and carrots – Pressure cook 8 to 10 minutes. Yield: 6 cups.

1 large onion, halved
3 medium rutabagas, diced
2 large turnips, diced
2 large carrots, chunks
½ cup water
¼ tsp. salt

Corn on the cob – Pressure cook 3 to 4 minutes.

4 ears corn
½ cup water
pinch salt

Combinations – All of these vegetables take 2 minutes to cook. Use singly or mix as you wish. Use ½ cup water and ⅛ tsp. salt per 4 cups vegetables.

---

green beans, whole
broccoli, flowerettes
cauliflower, flowerettes
greens, shredded
cabbage, shredded
Brussels sprouts, whole
yellow and zucchini squash, ½-inch rounds
onion, thin crescents

Comments – Pressure cooking vegetables saves time. Any vegetable can be pressure cooked. The smaller the vegetable is cut, the faster it will cook. Time carefully or the vegetables will turn out mushy. For information on using a pressure cooker, see page 239.

Stir-Fried Vegetables

Procedure – Heat oil in a pan over medium to medium-high heat. Saute onion until transparent. Add the first vegetable listed and saute briefly. Add remaining vegetables, one kind at a time, in the order listed. Saute each kind briefly before adding the next one. Add salt and water. Cover. Bring to a boil. Turn heat to low and simmer 10 to 15 minutes. Add soy sauce. If using a wok, see comments.

Butternut squash and kale – Yield: 6 to 7 cups.

1 tsp. sesame oil
1 medium onion, thin crescents
1 medium butternut squash, ½-inch squares
1 medium bunch kale;
    stems, thin diagonals
    leaves, 1-inch squares
¼ tsp. salt
½ cup water
½ tsp. soy sauce

Snowpeas and carrots with tofu – Marinate tofu in soy sauce while sauteing vegetables. Drain and reserve soy sauce. Add tofu after the last vegetable is sauteed. Cover and steam together 10 to 15 minutes over low heat. Use reserved soy sauce to season. Yield: 6 to 7 cups.

½ lb. tofu, ½-inch cubes
1 Tbsp. soy sauce
1 tsp. sesame oil
1 medium onion, thin crescents
3 medium carrots, large matchsticks
20 to 24 whole medium snowpeas
¼ tsp. salt
½ cup water

Yellow squash, cabbage, and carrots – Yield: 6 to 7 cups.

---

1 tsp. sesame oil
1 medium onion, thin crescents
1 medium carrot, thin matchsticks
3 medium yellow squash, paper cut
½ medium cabbage (core removed), shredded
½ cup water
¼ tsp. salt
½ tsp. soy sauce

Comments – Stir-frying produces crisp vegetables which retain their bright colors. Onions are cooked first, then remaining vegetables in yang to yin order. You can use as many vegetables as you like, but three are usually enough. Stir-frying works well in a wok or a regular pan. Either way requires almost constant stirring. Stir-fried vegetables are good served over rice.

If using a wok, note that when sauteing, vegetables in the middle receive most of the heat. Add vegetables to the middle of the pan and saute there. Push the sauteed vegetables to the side of the wok before adding the next vegetable so that the new vegetable will be in the middle of the wok, over the heat. Saute in the middle briefly, then mix with the already sauteed vegetables. Repeat the step of pushing to the side and adding the new vegetable to the middle until all the vegetables are sauteed. Add water and salt. Cover. Steam 7 to 10 minutes.

One variation is to use ginger. Add 2 to 3 teaspoons of freshly minced ginger to hot oil and saute very briefly, until fragrant. Add onion and continue with any of the combinations listed. Ginger adds flavor and balances well with the oil.

Another variation is to make sauce. Dilute 2 teaspoons arrowroot or kuzu in ¼ cup cold water. Add to vegetables after they have steamed. Cook until sauce becomes thick and transparent, about 1 minute. Add an extra ½ teaspoon soy sauce.

Sauteed Vegetables

Procedure – Heat oil in a pan. Saute onion with a pinch of salt until transparent. Add vegetables and the rest of the salt and saute 1 to 2 minutes. Stir often. (For more than one kind of vegetable, add in the order listed, each with some salt, sauteing after each addition.) Add the water. Cover. Bring to a boil. Simmer over low heat 20 to 25 minutes.

Broccoli – Yield: 5 to 6 cups.

½ tsp. sesame oil
1 medium onion, thin crescents
1 medium bunch broccoli;
    stems, thin diagonals
    2½-inch long flowerettes, ½-inch thick at stem
¼ tsp. salt
½ cup water

Greens and roots – Try turnip greens with turnips; collard greens with carrots; kale with rutabagas. Yield: 5 to 6 cups.

½ tsp. sesame oil
1 medium onion, thin crescents
1 medium bunch greens;
    stems, thin diagonals
    leaves, 1-inch squares
2 medium roots, diced
¼ tsp. salt
½ cup water

Carrots – Yield: 5 to 6 cups.

½ tsp. sesame oil
1 medium onion, thin crescents
4 medium carrots, large matchsticks
¼ tsp. salt
½ cup water

Celery and parsnips – Omit onion. Yield: 5 to 6 cups.

½ tsp. sesame oil
4 medium stalks celery, thin diagonals
4 medium parsnips, large matchsticks
¼ tsp. salt
½ cup water

Comments – This method is used for vegetables that contain less water, like roots and winter squash. Any vegetable may be prepared using this procedure. For extra flavor, add ¼ tsp. soy sauce at the end of cooking.

Sauteed Vegetables without Water

Procedure – Heat oil in a pan. Saute onion with a pinch of salt until transparent. Add vegetables and the rest of the salt and saute 1 to 2 minutes. Stir constantly. Cover. Simmer over low heat for the time indicated, or until tender, stirring once or twice.

Cabbage – Simmer 15 to 20 minutes. Yield: 5 to 6 cups.

1 tsp. sesame oil
1 medium onion, thin crescents
1 medium cabbage;
   core, finely minced
   leaves, 1-inch squares
¼ tsp. salt

Mustard greens – Simmer 10 to 15 minutes. Yield: 5 to 6 cups.

1 tsp. sesame oil
1 medium onion, thin crescents
1 medium bunch mustard greens;
   stems, finely minced
   leaves, shredded
¼ tsp. salt

Summer squash – Simmer 20 to 25 minutes. Yield: 7 to 8 cups.

1 tsp. sesame oil
1 medium onion, thin crescents
4 medium yellow squash, paper cut
4 medium zucchini, paper cut
½ tsp. salt

Comments – This method is used with vegetables that contain more water, like greens and summer squash. Sauteing with salt draws out water so the vegetables cook in their own juices. Also try Chinese cabbage or combinations such as mustard greens, onions, and carrots. For extra flavor, add ¼ tsp. soy sauce at the end of cooking.

Sauteed Vegetables with Soy Sauce

Procedure – Heat oil in a pan. Saute vegetables with salt, in the order listed, until fragrant, 1 to 2 minutes. Add water and soy sauce. Cover. Bring to a boil. Simmer 25 minutes over low heat. Uncover and cook until the remaining water evaporates.

Carrots – Yield: 4 to 5 cups.

1 tsp. sesame oil
1 medium onion, thin crescents
3 medium carrots, large matchsticks
⅛ tsp. salt
½ cup water
1 Tbsp. soy sauce

Rutabagas – Yield: 4 to 5 cups.

1 tsp. sesame oil
1 medium onion, minced
3 medium rutabagas, diced
⅛ tsp. salt
½ cup water
1 Tbsp. soy sauce

Burdock and carrots – Saute burdock 2 minutes, then add carrots. Yield: 6 to 7 cups.

2 tsp. sesame oil
3 small burdock, thin matchsticks
4 medium carrots, thin matchsticks
¼ tsp salt
¾ cup water
4 to 5 tsp. soy sauce

Comments – This method is used with root vegetables. Soy sauce creates a very flavorful dish.

Sauteed Vegetables with Miso

Procedure – Heat oil in a pan. Saute vegetables with salt, if used, until color changes, 1 to 2 minutes. Add water, if used. Cover. Bring to a boil. Simmer over low heat until tender, 10 to 15 minutes. Add miso in one lump. Cover and simmer 5 minutes to soften miso. Stir miso into the vegetables.

Scallion miso – Saute greens, then add whites. Yield: 3 cups.

2 tsp. sesame oil
4 bunches scallions;
   greens, thin rounds
   whites, thin rounds
4 to 5 tsp. dark miso (soybean, barley, or rice)

Onion miso – Yield: 4 cups.

2 tsp. sesame oil
4 medium onions, thin crescents
¼ tsp. salt
1 to 2 Tbsp. water
3 to 4 tsp. dark miso (soybean, barley, or rice)

Green pepper miso – Yield: 4 cups.

2 tsp. sesame oil
4 medium green peppers, thin crescents
4 to 5 tsp. dark miso (soybean, barley, or rice)

Comments – Vegetables cooked with miso make an appetizing side dish. Allow 2 to 3 tablespoons per serving. Scallions and green peppers will cook in their own juice, but onions need salt to draw out their juice. Miso is decreased when salt is added. Try cooking leeks or carrots with miso. Miso vegetables can be used as a spread or can be made into a mild vegetable dish by using less miso or a younger, lighter miso.

Simmered Vegetables

Procedure – Place water in a pan. Layer vegetables in the order listed. Sprinkle salt on top. Cover. Bring to a boil. Simmer for the time indicated over low heat.

Carrots – Simmer 20 to 30 minutes. Yield: 4 to 5 cups.

½ cup water
6 large carrots, big chunks or logs
¼ tsp. salt

Greens – Simmer 12 to 15 minutes. Yield: 4 to 5 cups.

½ cup water
1 bunch greens (kale, collards, etc.);
   stems, thin rounds
   leaves, 1-inch squares
pinch salt

Cabbage – Simmer 10 minutes. Yield: 4 to 5 cups.

½ cup water
1 medium cabbage (core removed), shredded
⅛ tsp. salt

Green beans, corn, and red onions – Simmer 10 to 15 minutes. Yield: 6 to 7 cups.

½ cup water
1 medium red onion, minced
20 medium green beans, ½-inch rounds
2 medium ears of corn, cut off the cob
¼ tsp. salt

Winter squash – Simmer 30 to 40 minutes. Yield: 4 to 5 cups.

1 cup water
1 large butternut or other squash, 2-inch squares
¼ tsp. salt

Sweet potatoes – Simmer 30 minutes to 2 hours – the longer the cooking time, the more flavorful. Yield: 5 to 7 cups.

1 to 1½ cups water
4 large sweet potatoes, large matchsticks or big chunks
½ tsp. salt

Comments – By simmering vegetables with salt on top, the salt is cooked into the vegetables. Most vegetables can be simmered with salt on top. The smaller the cuts, the faster the vegetables cook. Try combinations, too, layering from yin to yang.

Try adding nut or seed butter to cooked vegetables. Dilute 2 Tbsp. butter in ¼ cup hot water and add 1 tsp. soy sauce. Add to vegetables when they are tender. Cook until sauce is thick, 1 to 2 minutes, stirring constantly. Good with greens or broccoli.

Simmered Vegetables, Salted Water

Procedure – Bring water to a boil. Add salt. Add vegetables. Cover. Bring to a boil. Simmer for the time indicated over low heat.

Greens – Simmer stems 2 minutes, then add leaves and simmer 8 to 10 minutes. Yield: 4 to 5 cups.

> ½ cup water
> pinch salt
> 1 medium bunch greens (kale, collards, etc.);
>   stems, thin rounds
>   leaves, 1-inch squares

Broccoli – Simmer stems 3 minutes, then add flowerettes and simmer 10 to 12 minutes. Yield: 4 to 5 cups.

> ½ cup water
> ¼ tsp. salt
> 1 medium bunch broccoli;
>   stems, logs
>   3-inch long flowerettes, ½-inch thick at stem

Corn on the cob – Simmer 5 minutes.

> ½ cup water
> ⅛ tsp. salt
> 2 large ears of corn, 4-inch pieces

Comments – Cooking vegetables in salted water rather than sprinkling salt on top produces vegetables with less salt which are good for children and for summer cooking. Most vegetables can be cooked this way, singly or in combination. A vegetable steamer may be used; steam over gently boiling salted water for the same length of time.

Soups

Cooking – There are two basic ways to make soup. Boil all the ingredients together until tender, or saute all or some of the ingredients first and then boil until tender. Soups with sauteed ingredients are generally more flavorful. Boiled soups save time as they require only one utensil and can be made in minutes, as with instant soups, page 47.

Vegetables – Vegetables should be cooked until tender. Cut different vegetables into similar-sized pieces so the cooking time is the same. Larger cuts require longer cooking times; smaller and finer cuts cook faster. Vary the cuts for a pleasing appearance, using big cuts for stews and bite-sized cuts for other soups. Older vegetables cook well into soup; the longer cooking time makes them soft and flavorful. If you are in a hurry, use young vegetables because they cook quickly.

Pressure cooking – Many soups can be pressure cooked to save time. Follow the general pressure-cooking hints such as filling the cooker no more than two-thirds full and avoiding foods which may clog the cooker such as rolled oats, noodles, flour, tofu, dumplings, or wakame leaves. (Note: You may pressure cook the other ingredients and then simmer the dish after adding foods which should not be pressure cooked.) Follow the procedure to the "bring to a boil" stage. At that point, bring to full pressure. Pressure cook for one-third of the indicated time; for example, if the recipe calls for simmering 30 minutes, pressure cook for 10 minutes. For detailed information on using a pressure cooker, see page 239.

Seasoning with miso or soy sauce – Miso and soy sauce are fermented products and are better when just heated through and not boiled, so the beneficial bacteria are kept alive. Sometimes miso or soy sauce is cooked into a dish as in stews or condiments; but generally, for soups, it is added at the end of cooking and not boiled. Different kinds of miso can be used to season soup. I usually use a dark barley miso, aged about two years, in daily miso soup.

If making soup for more than one meal, it is a good idea to season only the portion to be served, either by ladling that amount into another pan for seasoning, or by seasoning the individual bowls. If soup is cooked with salt, it will need less seasoning than if it has no salt. Season soup to taste, and use either miso or soy sauce, not both. Dilute miso with ¼ cup hot broth, then mix with soup. Here are general proportions: For soups without salt (such as wakame or kombu soups), use 1 Tbsp. miso or 2 Tbsp. soy sauce per 4 cups soup. For soups with salt (such as sauteed or boiled vegetable soups), use 2 tsp. miso or 4 to 5 tsp. soy sauce per 4 cups soup.

These soups contain a basic flavoring of either miso or soy sauce. Small amounts of other seasonings such as herbs and spices may be added if you wish.

Instant Vegetable Soups

Procedure – Bring water to a boil. Add ingredients. Bring to a rolling boil. Remove from heat and season to taste.

Tofu, carrot, and scallion soup – Yield: 4 to 5 cups.

4 cups water
½ lb. tofu, ½-inch cubes
1 small carrot, finely grated
3 medium scallions, thin rounds
soy sauce or miso, see seasoning, page 46

Daikon, watercress, and nori soup – Yield: 4 to 5 cups.

4 cups water
1 cup finely grated daikon radish
½ cup minced watercress
1 sheet nori, roasted and torn into squares, page 78
soy sauce or miso, see seasoning, page 46

Comments – Soups can be made instantly when using foods that cook quickly like tofu, scallions, sprouts, dulse, couscous, or finely grated vegetables. Leftover foods such as cooked rice also can be added. Kombu soups cook quickly and use many of the same ingredients. See page 67.

Stews

Procedure – Measure water into a pan. Place kombu, if used, at the bottom. Layer vegetables from bottom to top in the order listed. Sprinkle salt on top. Cover. Bring to a boil. Simmer 45 minutes over low heat. Add soy sauce. Simmer another 15 minutes to cook soy sauce into the vegetables.

Potato, cabbage, and carrot stew – Yield: 12 to 14 cups.

> 4 cups water
> 4 medium red potatoes, halved
> 1 medium cabbage, 8 crescents
> 4 medium onions, quartered
> 4 medium carrots, large chunks
> ½ tsp. salt
> 2 Tbsp. soy sauce

Vegetable stew with kombu knots – Soak 4 six-inch pieces of kombu in 2 cups of water until pliable, 10 to 15 minutes. Slit each piece lengthwise into 1-inch wide strips. Tie each strip into a knot. Yield: 12 to 14 cups.

> 4 cups water (include reserved kombu soaking water)
> kombu knots
> 4 medium onions, quartered
> 4 medium rutabagas, quartered
> 2 medium daikon radishes, 2-inch rounds
> 4 medium carrots, large chunks
> ½ tsp. salt
> 2 Tbsp. soy sauce

Comments – A stew is both a vegetable dish and a soup. The vegetables can be served on a plate if desired, while the broth is served in a bowl. The vegetables are often root vegetables cut into large pieces. Layer vegetables from yin at the bottom to yang at the top. Kombu knots cook tender and are a pretty addition. Try other root vegetables in stews such as turnips or burdock. Stews pressure cook well, see page 45.

Boiled Vegetable Soups

Procedure – Layer vegetables from bottom to top in the order
listed. Add cold water. Sprinkle salt on top. Cover. Bring to a boil.
Simmer over low heat for the time indicated. Season to taste.

Celery, cabbage, and carrot soup – Simmer 30 minutes.
Yield: 8 to 10 cups.

---

    1 large celery stalk, thin quarter rounds
    1 small cabbage;
       core, finely minced
       leaves, shredded
    1 medium onion, minced
    1 medium carrot, thin quarter rounds
    6 to 8 cups water
    ¼ tsp. salt
    soy sauce, see seasoning, page 46

Vegetable soup with noodles and tofu – Simmer vegetables
15 minutes. Add noodles and simmer 15 minutes. Add tofu and
simmer another 5 minutes. Season. Yield: 10 to 12 cups.

---

    1 medium butternut squash, 1-inch squares
    1 large onion, thin crescents
    1 medium carrot, shaved
    8 to 10 cups water
    ½ tsp. salt
    1 cup whole wheat ribbon noodles
    ½ lb. tofu, ½-inch cubes
    soy sauce, see seasoning, page 46

Yellow squash, scallion, and nori quick soup – Simmer 5 to 7 minutes. Garnish with scallions and nori when serving soup. Yield: 4 to 5 cups.

---

2 small yellow squash, thin quarter rounds
4 cups water
⅛ tsp. salt
miso or soy sauce, see seasoning, page 46
garnish:
    1 medium scallion, thin rounds
    1 sheet nori, matchsticks, page 78

Comments – Many different soups can be made from this general procedure. Just layer vegetables from yin at the bottom to yang at the top. Boil until tender, adding whatever is desired (noodles, tofu, dumplings, garnishes). Soup can be made more quickly from young, finely cut vegetables. Other combinations include green beans and tofu as a quick soup; yellow squash, carrots, and noodles garnished with scallions and croutons; and broccoli and fresh corn with dumplings.

Boiled Vegetable Soups, Creamy

Procedure – Layer vegetables from bottom to top in the order listed. Add cold water. Sprinkle salt on top. Cover. Bring to a boil. Simmer for the time indicated over low heat. Dilute nut or seed butter in ½ cup of the hot soup broth. Add to soup with the seasoning. Stir to heat through but do not boil.

Creamy cauliflower soup with dumplings – Simmer core for 10 minutes. Add flowerettes and simmer 15 minutes. Add dumplings and simmer 5 minutes. Yield: 8 to 9 cups.

> 1 medium cauliflower;
>   core, finely minced
>   2-inch long flowerettes, ½-inch thick at stem
> 6 cups water
> ¼ tsp. salt
> 30 to 35 whole wheat dumplings, page 156
> 2 Tbsp. sesame butter
> 4 tsp. light miso or 2 to 3 Tbsp. soy sauce

Creamy macaroni soup – Simmer vegetables for 10 minutes. Add macaroni and simmer 15 minutes. Yield: 8 to 10 cups.

> 1 medium onion, minced
> 1 cup fresh green peas
> 1 medium carrot, thin flowers
> 8 cups water
> ¼ tsp. salt
> 1 cup whole wheat elbow macaroni
> 2 Tbsp. sesame butter or almond butter
> 2 to 4 Tbsp. soy sauce

Comments – Creamy boiled soup is a variation on the basic boiled soup. Diluted nut or seed butter is added to make it creamy. Try broccoli and noodles; or carrots garnished with parsley.

Sauteed Vegetable Soups

Procedure – Heat water in a kettle. Heat oil in a pan and saute onion with a pinch of salt until transparent (or saute leek greens until bright green). Add vegetables in the order listed, one kind at a time. Saute each kind for 1 to 2 minutes. Add boiling water. Sprinkle remaining salt on top. Cover. Bring to a boil. Simmer for the time indicated over low heat. Season to taste.

Onion soup with croutons – Saute onions for 5 minutes for increased flavor. Simmer soup 30 to 35 minutes. Serve with croutons or over cooked noodles. Yield: 8 to 10 cups.

> 2 tsp. sesame oil
> 5 medium onions, thin crescents
> 6 to 8 cups water
> ½ tsp. salt
> soy sauce or miso, see seasoning, page 46
> garnish: croutons, page 195

Broccoli and tofu soup with dumplings – Saute onion and then broccoli stems. Add water and simmer 10 minutes. Add flowerettes. Simmer 15 minutes. Add tofu and dumplings and simmer 5 minutes. Season. Yield: 8 to 10 cups.

> 1 tsp. sesame oil
> 1 medium onion, thin crescents
> 1 medium bunch broccoli;
>   stems, thin quarter rounds
>   2-inch long broccoli flowerettes, ½-inch thick at stem
> 6 cups water
> ¼ tsp. salt
> 30 to 35 whole wheat dumplings, page 156
> ½ lb. tofu, ½-inch cubes
> soy sauce, see seasoning, page 46

Leek and squash soup – Simmer 30 to 35 minutes. Yield: 8 to 10 cups.

½ tsp. sesame oil
3 medium leeks;
   greens, thin rounds
   whites, thin rounds
1 medium butternut squash, ½-inch squares
6 to 8 cups water
¼ tsp. salt
soy sauce, see seasoning, page 46

Comments – Many different soups can be made from this general procedure. Just saute the vegetables, add water and salt, and simmer until tender, adding whatever is desired (noodles, tofu, dumplings, garnishes). For other combinations, try onion, green beans, yellow squash, and carrots; or winter squash and dumplings. Garnish with scallions and nori. All sauteed soups in this section are variations of this basic procedure.

Sauteed Vegetable Soups, Pureed

Procedure – Heat water in a kettle. Heat oil in a pan and saute onion with a pinch of salt until transparent. Add vegetables in the order listed, one kind at a time. Saute each kind for 1 to 2 minutes. Add boiling water. Sprinkle remaining salt on top. Cover. Bring to a boil. Simmer 30 minutes over low heat. Puree in a blender or a food mill, mash as smooth as possible with a masher, or press through a sieve. Bring to a boil. Add soy sauce to taste. Garnish when serving, if desired.

Creamy squash soup – Yield: 10 cups.

1 tsp. sesame oil
1 large onion, minced
1 large butternut squash, 1-inch squares
8 cups water
¼ tsp. salt
soy sauce, see seasoning, page 46
garnish: croutons, page 195

Creamy beets and carrot soup – Yield: 8 to 10 cups.

1 tsp. sesame oil
1 medium onion, thin crescents
4 medium beets, diced
2 medium carrots, thin quarter rounds
6 to 8 cups water
¼ tsp. salt
soy sauce, see seasoning, page 46

Comments – Pureed soups are variations on the basic sauteed soup, pureeing vegetables after they are cooked tender. Other pureed soup combinations include onion, winter squash, and carrots; or potatoes and yellow squash.

Sauteed Vegetable Soups with Noodles

Procedure - Heat water in a kettle. Heat oil in a pan and saute onion with a pinch of salt until transparent. Add vegetables in the order listed, one kind at a time. Saute each kind for 1 to 2 minutes. Add boiling water. Sprinkle remaining salt on top. Cover. Bring to a boil. Simmer 15 to 20 minutes. Add noodles and simmer 15 more minutes. Add seasoning to taste.

Celery and cabbage soup with noodles - Yield 10 to 12 cups.

1 tsp. sesame oil
1 medium onion, thin crescents
2 large celery stalks, thin diagonals
½ medium cabbage;
    core, minced
    leaves, shredded
8 to 10 cups water
½ tsp. salt
1 cup whole wheat ribbon noodles
soy sauce, see seasoning, page 46

Tomato, zucchini, and macaroni soup - Simmer vegetables for 30 minutes. Add macaroni and simmer 15 more minutes. Note: This soup is particularly good the next day. Yield: 10 to 12 cups.

1 tsp. sesame oil
1 medium onion, minced
1 large tomato, diced
3 medium zucchini, quarter rounds
8 to 10 cups water
½ tsp. salt
1 cup whole wheat elbow macaroni
soy sauce, see seasoning, page 46

Comments – Noodles can be cooked into almost any kind of soup. Follow the basic procedure adding water if necessary. Always add noodles during the last 15 minutes of simmering. Try these combinations: onion, winter squash, carrots, and whole wheat ribbon noodles, garnished with scallions; or onion, celery, buckwheat noodles (broken into small pieces), and tofu. Other soups with noodles are listed in the index.

Sauteed Vegetable Soups with Grain

Procedure – Heat water in a kettle. Heat oil in a pan and saute onion with a pinch of salt until transparent. Add vegetables in the order listed, one kind at a time. Saute each kind for 1 to 2 minutes. Add boiling water. Place grain on top of the vegetables. Sprinkle remaining salt on top of the grain. Cover. Bring to a boil. Simmer for the time indicated over low heat, until grain is soft. Season with soy sauce to taste.

Oatmeal and celery soup – Simmer 30 minutes. Yield: 8 to 10 cups.

---

1 tsp. sesame oil
1 large onion, thin crescents
4 large celery stalks, thin diagonals
8 cups water
1 cup rolled oats
¼ tsp. salt
soy sauce, see seasoning, page 46

Rice, turnip, and carrot soup – Wash and drain rice. Roast in a dry skillet (no oil) until browned and popped, 10 to 15 minutes. Simmer soup 1 to 1½ hours. Yield: 10 to 12 cups.

---

1 tsp. sesame oil
1 medium onion, minced
3 medium turnips, diced
1 medium carrot, thin quarter rounds
8 to 10 cups water
1 cup rice, roasted
¼ tsp. salt
soy sauce, see seasoning, page 46

Comments – Vegetable soup with grain is a variation on the basic sauteed soup with the addition of grain which is cooked with the vegetables. Try other grains such as barley or millet, or try soaking (instead of roasting) the grain for 1 hour before adding to soup. Tofu can be added during the last 5 minutes. Or, noodles can be added during the last 15 minutes to make a hearty one-pot meal. A good combination is onion, celery, carrots, millet, and noodles. Soups with whole grains pressure cook well and are very flavorful, see page 45.

Sauteed Vegetable Soups with Arrowroot

Procedure – Heat water in a kettle. Heat oil in a pan and saute onion with a pinch of salt until transparent. Add vegetables in the order listed, one kind at a time. Saute each kind for 1 to 2 minutes. Add boiling water. Sprinkle remaining salt on top. Cover. Bring to a boil. Simmer 20 to 25 minutes over low heat. Add dissolved arrowroot or kuzu and stir, simmering until soup is clear and creamy, 1 to 2 minutes. Season to taste.

> **Creamy corn and green bean soup** – Yield: 8 to 10 cups.
>
> ½ tsp. sesame oil
> 1 large onion, minced
> 16 large green beans, ½-inch rounds
> 2 medium ears of corn, cut off the cob
> 6 cups water
> ¼ tsp. salt
> 2 to 3 Tbsp. arrowroot or kuzu dissolved in ½ cup
>   cold water
> light miso or soy sauce, see seasoning, page 46

Comments – Creamy arrowroot soups are variations on the basic sauteed soup, adding dissolved arrowroot after vegetables have cooked tender. Other combinations include onion, celery, winter squash and carrots; and onion, green peas, and tofu.

Sauteed Vegetable Soups with Flour

Procedure – Heat water in a kettle. Heat oil in a pan and saute onion with a pinch of salt until transparent (or saute leek greens until bright green). Add vegetables in the order listed, one kind at a time. Saute each kind for 1 to 2 minutes. Add flour and roast with the vegetables until fragrant, 2 to 3 minutes, stirring constantly. Flour will coat the vegetables. Remove from heat. Add boiling water, using a whisk to smooth lumps. Place over medium heat. Add salt. Cover. Bring to a boil. Simmer 30 minutes over low heat. Season to taste.

Creamy leek soup – Yield: 10 cups.

2 tsp. sesame oil
3 large leeks;
    greens, thin rounds
    whites, thin rounds
1 cup whole wheat flour or brown rice flour
8 cups boiling water
¼ tsp. salt
light miso or soy sauce, see seasoning, page 46

Creamy cornmeal soup – Yield: 10 cups.

2 tsp. sesame oil
1 medium onion, thin crescents
3 medium celery stalks, thin quarter rounds
2 medium carrots, thin quarter rounds or flowers
1 cup cornmeal
8 cups boiling water
¼ tsp. salt
soy sauce, see seasoning, page 46

Comments – Creamy soup with flour is a variation on the basic sauteed soup, roasting flour with sauteed vegetables and then adding boiling water. Other combinations include onion and celery with buckwheat flour; and onion and rutabaga with brown rice flour and garnished with parsley.

Miso Soups with Wakame, Boiled

Procedure – Soak wakame in cold water until soft, 10 to 15 minutes. Drain and reserve soaking water. Separate leaves from stems and cut each as directed. In a pot, layer wakame stems and vegetables in the order listed. Add reserved soaking water and cold water to equal the amount called for, being careful not to disturb layers. Cover. Bring to a boil. Simmer 40 minutes over low heat. Add wakame leaves and simmer 5 minutes more. Season with miso.

Cabbage, turnip, and wakame miso soup – Yield: 8 to 9 cups.

6-inch strip of wakame, soaked in 2 cups water;
    stems, thin rounds
    leaves, ½-inch squares
½ small cabbage;
    core, finely minced
    leaves, shredded
2 medium turnips, diced
6 to 8 cups water (include reserved soaking water)
miso, see seasoning, page 46

Daikon radish, scallion, and wakame miso soup – Garnish with scallions when serving. Yield: 8 to 9 cups.

6-inch strip of wakame, soaked in 2 cups water;
    stems, thin rounds
    leaves, ½-inch squares
1 small daikon radish, thin quarter rounds
6 to 8 cups water (include reserved soaking water)
miso, see seasoning, page 46
garnish: scallions, thin rounds

Comments – Boiling wakame into soup is a variation on the basic boiled vegetable soup; just place softened, chopped wakame stems at the bottom of the pan and layer vegetables from yin at the bottom to yang at the top. Salt is omitted. The soup is simmered 45 minutes so the wakame stems become tender. The leaves are tender and need only 5 minutes of cooking. Wakame and miso complement each other and produce a hearty nutritious soup. Any vegetable can be used, but since the soup simmers 45 minutes, roots and older vegetables work the best. Use one, two, or three kinds of vegetables. Try cabbage with rutabagas; or cauliflower leaves, cabbage hearts, or broccoli stems with onion and carrots.

Miso soup can be made by following procedures such as Boiled Vegetable Soups, page 50; and Instant Vegetable Soups, page 47.

Miso Soups with Wakame, Sauteed

Procedure – Heat water in a kettle. Soak wakame in cold water until softened, 10 to 15 minutes. Drain and reserve soaking water. Separate leaves from stems and cut each as directed. Heat oil in a pan and saute onion until transparent. Add vegetables in the order listed, one kind at a time. Saute each kind until fragrant, 1 to 2 minutes. Place wakame stems on top of the vegetables. Add reserved soaking water and boiling water to equal amount called for, being careful not to disturb layers. Cover. Bring to a boil. Simmer 40 minutes. Add wakame leaves and simmer another 5 minutes. Season with miso.

Bok choy, carrot, and wakame miso soup – Yield: 10 to 12 cups.

6-inch strip of wakame, soaked in 2 cups water;
    stems, thin rounds
    leaves, ½-inch squares
1 tsp. sesame oil
1 large onion, thin crescents
1 medium bok choy;
    whites, thin quarter rounds
    greens, 1-inch squares
1 small carrot, shaved
8 to 10 cups water, (include reserved soaking water)
miso, see seasoning, page 46

Squash, turnip, and wakame miso soup – Yield: 10 to 12 cups.

6-inch strip of wakame, soaked in 2 cups water;
    stems, thin rounds
    leaves, ½-inch squares
1 tsp. sesame oil
1 large onion, thin crescents
½ small butternut squash, ½-inch squares
3 small turnips, diced
8 to 10 cups water (include reserved soaking water)
miso, see seasoning, page 46

Comments – This procedure is a variation on the basic sauteed vegetable soup. Vegetables are sauteed and then boiled with softened, chopped wakame. Try other vegetables for different kinds of miso soup, using one, two, or three kinds of vegetables. Winter squash goes well with daikon radish, burdock root, or beets. Summer squash goes well with cabbage, carrots, large green beans, or cabbage hearts. Try a simple soup of only one vegetable, like turnips or cabbage. Also, try cooking millet into soup; place ¼ cup washed and drained millet on top of the vegetables. Increase the water by 2 cups.

Clear Broths with Kombu

Procedure – Place kombu and shiitake mushrooms, if used, in cold water. Cover. Bring to a rolling boil. Remove ingredients immediately. Add soy sauce.

Kombu clear soup – Yield: 4 cups.

4-inch piece of kombu
4 cups cold water
2 Tbsp. soy sauce

Kombu and shiitake mushroom clear soup – Yield: 4 cups.

4-inch piece of kombu
2 medium shiitake mushrooms
4 cups cold water
2 Tbsp. soy sauce

Comments – Clear soup is easy to make and very flavorful. It is a good choice to serve with holiday or fancy meals. For serving with cooked noodles, increase soy sauce by 1 Tbsp. for more flavor. Soups can be garnished when serving to add flavor or balance to a meal. Try thin rounds of scallions or minced parsley; grated carrot or radish; nori roasted and cut into matchsticks, page 78; or a thin quarter slice of lemon, one per bowl.

Kombu and shiitake mushrooms are used without soaking. When brought to a boil, the flavor is drawn out. Don't boil too long, or soup may become bitter. They can be used again to make a second broth. Place in cold water, bring to a boil, and simmer for 15 minutes. Remove. Leftover kombu and shiitake mushrooms may be used in sea vegetable dishes, page 74.

Kombu Soups with Vegetables

Procedure - Placc kombu and shiitake mushrooms, if used, in cold water. Cover. Bring to a rolling boil. Remove kombu (and mushrooms). Add vegetables and tofu, if used. Bring to a rolling boil again. If using egg, add next, stirring soup constantly while adding. Add soy sauce.

Kombu clear soup with tofu and scallions - Yield: 4 to 5 cups.

4 cups cold water
4-inch piece kombu
½ lb. tofu, ½-inch cubes
4 medium scallions, thin diagonals
2 Tbsp. soy sauce

Kombu and shiitake mushroom soup with egg and watercress - Yield: 4 to 5 cups.

4 cups cold water
4-inch piece kombu
2 medium shiitake mushrooms
½ cup minced watercress
1 medium egg, beaten
2 Tbsp. soy sauce

Comments - Kombu soup with vegetables is easy to make. It is good served over cooked buckwheat noodles (increase soy sauce by 1 Tbsp.) and/or fried fish, see page 98. Try other combinations such as kombu soup with shredded Chinese cabbage, scallions, and egg; or kombu soup with tofu and minced alfalfa sprouts.

Vegetable Soups with Fish

Procedure – Heat water in a kettle. Heat oil in a pan and saute onion with a pinch of salt until transparent. Add vegetables in the order listed, one kind at a time. Saute each kind for 1 to 2 minutes. Add boiling water. Sprinkle remaining salt on top. Cover. Bring to a boil. Simmer 30 minutes over low heat. Add fish. Simmer another 4 to 5 minutes. Add diluted arrowroot, if used, and stir until clear and creamy, 1 to 2 minutes. Season with soy sauce.

Potato, squash, and fish soup – Yield: 6 to 8 cups.

½ tsp. sesame oil
1 large onion, minced
2 medium red potatoes, diced
2 medium yellow squash, quarter rounds
4 to 6 cups water
¼ tsp. salt
½ lb. fish fillets, 1-inch pieces
soy sauce, see seasoning, page 46

Creamy mushroom and fish soup – Yield: 6 cups.

½ tsp. sesame oil
1 large onion, minced
12 large mushrooms, thin lengthwise slices
4 cups water
¼ tsp. salt
½ lb. fish fillets, 1-inch pieces
1 Tbsp. arrowroot diluted in ¼ cup cold water
soy sauce, see seasoning, page 46

Comments – Vegetable soups with fish are a variation on the basic sauteed soup, with fish added during the last 5 minutes of simmering. For variety, cook dumplings or noodles into soup. Try leeks, potatoes, noodles, and fish; or onion, okra, fresh corn, and fish.

Sea Vegetables

Using sea vegetables – Sea vegetables are high in minerals and add important nutrients to a grain-based diet. Sea vegetables can be used in a variety of ways, from soups to bean dishes to desserts. When used by themselves, sea vegetables are usually served in small amounts.

Rehydrating – Sea vegetables are usually purchased in dried form. Some (like nori and dulse) can be used as purchased, while others (like hijiki and arame) need to be rehydrated (soaked until softened) before using. Different brands yield different quantities when softened. Some brands are more expensive but yield more when softened than less expensive brands. Hijiki varies considerably. Check packaging. Recipes included here call for amounts both in the dry form and in the rehydrated form. If you end up with more or less of the rehydrated sea vegetable than called for, cook it anyway; the dish will turn out fine.

Washing – Nori, agar-agar, kombu, and wakame usually don't need washing. Hijiki, arame, and dulse need to be cleaned. Procedures include washing instructions.

Cooking – Generally, the more processed the sea vegetable, the faster it cooks (like agar-agar). Soy sauce is used in most sea vegetable dishes to make the dish more delicious.

Hijiki

Procedure – Soak hijiki in water to cover until softened, 10 to 15 minutes. Drain and reserve soaking water. Then wash: Put drained, softened hijiki in a big bowl. Add water to cover. Pour only the hijiki that floats into a sieve without pouring off all the water or hijiki. Add more water and pour off floating hijiki again without pouring off all the water. Repeat with remaining hijiki until all the hijiki has floated and has been poured into the sieve. Sand will have settled to the bottom of the bowl for discarding. Repeat the whole process of washing. Drain.

Heat oil in a pan. Add ingredients in the order listed, one kind at a time. Saute each kind for 1 to 2 minutes. Add reserved soaking water (except for the bottom residue which may contain sand) and extra water to equal the amount called for. Add soy sauce. Cover and leave lid ajar. Bring to a boil. Simmer 20 to 30 minutes over low heat. Remove cover. Cook away any remaining liquid.

Hijiki with carrots and sesame seeds – Yield: 3 to 4 cups.

2 tsp. sesame oil
¼ cup sesame seeds, washed and drained
2 large carrots, thin matchsticks
½ cup hijiki, soaked in 2 cups water; will swell to 2 cups
1 cup water (include reserved soaking water)
2 Tbsp. soy sauce

Hijiki with peanuts – Yield: 2 to 3 cups.

2 tsp. sesame oil
¼ cup raw Spanish peanuts, washed and drained
½ cup hijiki, soaked in 2 cups water; will swell to 2 cups
1 cup water (include reserved soaking water)
2 Tbsp. soy sauce

Hijiki with tempeh – Yield: 3 to 4 cups.

2 tsp. sesame oil
1 large onion, thin crescents
½ cup hijiki, soaked in 2 cups water; will swell to 2 cups
4 oz. tempeh, ½-inch cubes
1 cup water (include reserved soaking water)
2 to 3 Tbsp. soy sauce

Comments – Because hijiki grows in shallow water and collects sand, it must be washed well. All brands contain sand; some more than others. This method of soaking before washing allows the hijiki to soften first so the sand will separate. Then, when washing, some of the water is left in the bowl. The sand will settle to the bottom rather than be poured out with the hijiki. Don't take short cuts when washing hijiki. It may seem faster merely to rinse the hijiki quickly before rehydrating; however, a quick rinse will not remove the sand.

Arame is similar to hijiki in appearance but has a milder flavor. It grows in 12-inch-long fronds, and is cut into matchsticks before packaging.

Try adding cooked noodles to any of the recipes for variety: Cook dish with 1 tablespoon more soy sauce; cool, then mix with 4 cups cooled, cooked noodles. Hijiki and arame can be substituted for each other in any of the listed recipes.

Arame

Procedure – Soak arame in water to cover until softened, 5 to 10 minutes. Drain and reserve soaking water. Wash arame in the same way as hijiki, one time only, page 70.

Heat oil in a pan. Add ingredients in the order listed, one kind at a time. Saute each kind for 1 to 2 minutes, before adding the next one. Add reserved soaking water and extra water to equal the amount called for. Add soy sauce. Cover and leave lid ajar. Bring to a boil. Simmer 20 to 25 minutes over low heat. Remove cover. Cook away remaining liquid.

Arame with green beans and carrots – Yield: 4 to 5 cups.

2 tsp. sesame oil
1 large onion, thin crescents
1 cup arame, soaked in 2 cups water; will swell to 2 cups
12 large green beans, thin diagonals
2 large carrots, thin matchsticks
1 cup water (include reserved soaking water)
2 Tbsp. soy sauce

Arame with carrots and peanut sauce – Cook arame with all ingredients except peanut butter for 25 minutes. Add diluted peanut butter and cook 5 minutes. Yield: 3 to 4 cups.

2 tsp. sesame oil
1 large onion, thin crescents
1 cup arame, soaked in 2 cups water; will swell to 2 cups
2 large carrots, thin matchsticks
1 cup water (include reserved soaking water)
2 Tbsp. soy sauce
2 Tbsp. peanut butter, diluted in 2 Tbsp. hot water

Comments – See comments under Hijiki, page 71.

Dulse

Procedure – Gently sort through dulse to remove any shells or rocks. Soak 5 minutes in water to cover. Drain and reserve soaking water. Heat oil in pan. Add ingredients in the order listed, one kind at a time. Saute each kind for 1 to 2 minutes, before adding the next one. Add reserved soaking water and extra water to equal needed amount. Add soy sauce. Cover. Bring to a boil. Simmer 20 to 25 minutes. Remove cover. Cook away remaining liquid.

Dulse with carrots and onions – Yield: 1 to 2 cups.

1 tsp. sesame oil
1 large onion, thin crescents
¼ cup dulse, soaked in ½ cup water; will swell to ½ cup
1 large carrot, thin matchsticks
1 cup water (include reserved soaking water)
1 Tbsp. soy sauce

Dulse with potatoes – Yield: 2 to 3 cups.

1 tsp. sesame oil
1 large onion, minced
4 medium red potatoes, diced
¼ cup dulse, soaked in ½ cup water, will swell to ½ cup
1 cup water (include reserved soaking water)
4 to 5 tsp. soy sauce

Comments – Dulse grows in shallow water. Sometimes there are shells or rocks clinging to the leaves. Clean before soaking. Dulse is a delicate sea vegetable and is easier to handle when dry than when wet. Try cooking dulse with onion and rutabaga.

Kombu and Nori

Procedure – Soak sea vegetables and shiitake mushrooms, if used, in water to cover until softened: Sea vegetables, 10 to 15 minutes; shiitake mushrooms, 20 to 25 minutes. Soak each kind in its own bowl. For kombu and mushrooms; drain, reserve soaking water(s), and slice as directed. Place all ingredients (including reserved soaking water) in a pan. Cover. Bring to a boil. Simmer until tender over low heat, with lid ajar, 30 to 40 minutes. Remove cover. Simmer away remaining liquid.

Kombu with soy sauce – Yield: ½ cup.

4-inch piece of kombu, soaked in 1 cup water; cut into thin matchsticks after soaking
1 Tbsp. soy sauce

Nori with soy sauce – Yield: 2 to 3 cups.

1 pkg. (10 sheets) nori, torn into 1-inch squares and soaked in 2 cups water
2 to 3 Tbsp. soy sauce

Kombu and shiitake mushrooms – Yield: 1 to 2 cups.

4-inch piece kombu, soaked in 1 cup water; cut into thin matchsticks after soaking
2 medium shiitake mushrooms, soaked in 1 cup water; cut after soaking;
    stems, diced (discard hard uncuttable part)
    caps, thin crescents
2 to 3 Tbsp. soy sauce

Kombu and nori – Yield: 3 to 4 cups.

4-inch piece kombu, soaked in 1 cup water, cut into thin
   matchsticks after soaking
1 pkg. (10 sheets) nori, torn into 1-inch squares and
   soaked in 2 cups water
3 to 4 Tbsp. soy sauce

Comments – Use sea vegetables boiled with soy sauce as a salty condiment. They will keep 7 to 10 days. These recipes can be made from kombu or shiitake mushrooms left over from making soup. In this case, use half the water but the full amount of soy sauce called for.

Wakame Salads

Procedure – Soak wakame 10 minutes in water to cover. Drain. Separate leaves from stems. Chop leaves into ½-inch pieces. (Reserve stems and soaking water for another use.) Mix dressing. Mix ingredients into the dressing in the order listed, one kind at a time.

Wakame and cucumber salad – Yield: 2 to 3 cups.

Dressing: use mixed dressing procedure, page 115
    1 Tbsp. light miso
    2 Tbsp. sesame butter
    ½ large lemon, juiced
2 six-inch pieces of wakame, soaked in 2 cups water;
    will swell to ½ cup
2 medium cucumbers, thin half rounds

Wakame, cucumber, and lettuce salad – Yield: 3 to 4 cups.

Dressing: use mixed dressing procedure, page 115
    2 Tbsp. brown rice vinegar
    2 Tbsp. soy sauce
2 six-inch pieces of wakame, soaked in 2 cups water;
    will swell to ½ cup
1 medium cucumber, thin quarter rounds
1 small (or ½ medium) lettuce, torn into bite-sized squares

Comments – Wakame leaves can be eaten without cooking, but the stems need to be cooked because they are hard. After soaking wakame for salads, save the stems and soaking water for soup. Also try wakame leaves with lettuce, scallions, and celery with a heated oil and soy sauce dressing.

Dulse Salads

Procedure – Gently sort through dulse to remove any shells or rocks. Soak dulse for 5 minutes in liquid to be used in dressing. Then mix in sesame butter if used. Mix salad ingredients into dressing in the order listed, one kind at a time.

Carrot, celery, cucumber, and dulse salad – Yield: 2 to 3 cups.

Dressing:
  ¼ cup dulse
  1 Tbsp. lemon juice
  1 Tbsp. soy sauce
  1 Tbsp. soft sesame butter
1 medium carrot, grated
3 small celery stalks, diced
1 medium cucumber, thin quarter rounds

Cucumber, celery, walnut, and dulse salad – Yield: 2 to 3 cups.

Dressing:
  ¼ cup dulse
  2 tsp. lemon juice
  2 tsp. soy sauce
½ cup roasted walnuts, chopped, page 127
2 small celery stalks, diced
2 medium cucumbers, quarter rounds

Comments – If dulse is added to a salad it often falls apart when it becomes wet, so in these recipes it is mixed into the dressing. Try soaking dulse in any of the Mixed Salad Dressings (page 115) and mix in with lettuce salads.

Garnishes

Nori, roasted – Roast one sheet of nori by holding it 1 to 2 inches above a low flame or medium-high heat on an electric stove. Pass it back and forth. Roast 1 side only. In 1 to 2 minutes nori will turn green and smell fragrant. The texture will be crinkled. Crush, or tear into squares.

Nori, matchsticks – Using scissors, cut one sheet of nori in half lengthwise along fold. Cut each half again in half lengthwise. Lay these 4 strips on top of each other. Cut across into very thin matchsticks.

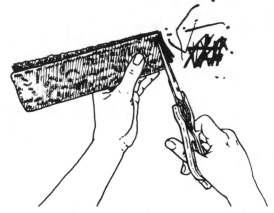

Wakame, roasted – Place dry wakame leaves (no soaking) in dry skillet (no oil). Roast over medium to low flame 15 to 20 minutes. Wakame will brown, smell fragrant, and turn crispy. Eat as is or grind to a fine powder in blender or suribachi. Roasted wakame keeps well. It can be ground with roasted sesame seeds, page 127.

Dulse, roasted – Gently sort through dulse to remove any shells or rocks. Flatten dry dulse (do not soak) and place in a dry skillet (no oil). Roast over medium to low heat until dulse is fragrant and crispy, 5 to 7 minutes. Crush or eat as is. Note: Dulse can be eaten raw, but is more flavorful when roasted. It resembles chips.

Beans

Preparations – Dry beans add protein, flavor, and variety to a grain-based diet. However, many people find beans hard to digest. Some beans may cause more gas than others, but usually gas results when beans aren't properly cooked. To prevent gas by making them easier to assimilate, follow these tips: soak beans; use kombu; pressure cook or boil until completely soft, then add salt and cook it into the beans; spice naturally and minimally. In preparing bean dishes, there are two steps – pre-cooking until soft by pressure cooking (page 81) or boiling (page 82), and then following any of the procedures using beans.

Cleaning and washing – Sort through beans carefully before washing to remove dirt and rocks. Go through them in small amounts, especially the big beans. To wash, put beans in a pot, add water, swish, and drain. Repeat.

Soaking – Soaking before cooking allows the beans to swell so they will cook thoroughly. Soak with kombu in the full quantity of water required for cooking. Larger beans require longer soaking times. Or, save time by putting washed beans, kombu, and water in a pressure cooker. Bring to full pressure, and remove from heat. Let stand 1 hour, then cook until soft.

Adding kombu – Kombu adds minerals to beans and helps cook them more thoroughly. After washing beans, add water and kombu,

79

then soak. When cooking, the kombu will become soft. It can then be mashed easily into the beans or it may be removed.

Adding salt – Cook beans until soft before adding salt. If salt is added early, beans will not become soft. Salt brings out the flavor of the beans. After adding salt, cook beans at least 30 minutes so salt is cooked into the beans.

Cutting and adding vegetables – Cut vegetables into bite-sized pieces for bean dishes, using various cuts of similar size for different vegetables. Cutting pieces slightly larger than the bean size makes an attractive dish. Most bean dishes are better if the beans are cooked until soft before adding vegetables. The beans will be cooked thoroughly and the vegetables will be tender but not mushy. Add the vegetables and cook at least 30 minutes.

Seasoning – Most bean dishes are cooked with salt. Soy sauce, miso, or other seasoning may be added just before serving to enhance the flavor. If you are cooking a large quantity of beans, season only the portion to be served. Here are general proportions: use 2 to 3 tsp. soy sauce or 1 to 2 tsp. miso per 4 cups of any bean dish. Bean dishes cooked with miso need no extra seasoning. Occasionally, chili, curry powder, bay leaves, or basil, etc., makes a nice addition. Be careful not to over-spice; too much spice can cause gas. Avoid herbs and spices with preservatives or other additives.

Using cooked beans – Beans may be served as soups, sauces, or side dishes. The recipes in this section can be changed by altering the amount of water and serving in a different style. Soups can be made into sauces, or side dishes can be made into soups. Also, a leftover bean dish can be transformed into a new dish by adding more water or thickening with grain, noodles, or arrowroot. Or, cooked vegetables can be combined with cooked beans.

Pressure Cooking Beans

Procedure – Sort through beans. Wash and drain. Soak with kombu in the full amount of water. Cover. Place over medium to medium-high heat and bring to full pressure (15 lbs.). Slip a flame tamer under the cooker and turn heat to low. Cook for the time indicated at full pressure.

Large beans – Chickpeas, pinto beans, kidney beans, black turtle beans, great northern beans. Soak 6 to 8 hours. Pressure cook 45 minutes. Yield: 4 to 5 cups.

2 cups beans
4-inch piece of kombu
4 cups water

Medium beans – Navy beans, lima beans, black-eyed peas. Soak 4 to 6 hours. Pressure cook 30 minutes. Yield: 4 to 5 cups.

2 cups beans
4-inch piece of kombu
4 cups water

Comments – Pressure cooking uses less time and water than boiling. It also increases the flavor. Not all beans can be pressure cooked, though. Do not pressure cook lentils, split peas, or soybeans as they may clog the cooker vent. Boil azuki beans for best flavor; they can become bitter if pressure cooked. Soak beans, cook until soft, and then use one of the procedures for boiled or sauteed dishes. For more information on using a pressure cooker, see page 239.

Boiling Beans

Procedure – Sort through beans. Wash and drain. Soak with kombu in the full amount of water. Cover. Bring to a boil. Simmer for the time indicated over low heat, with lid ajar if necessary to prevent spillover.

Large beans – Chickpeas, pinto beans, kidney beans, etc. Soak 6 to 8 hours. Boil 2 to 2½ hours. Yield: 4 to 5 cups.

2 cups beans
4-inch piece of kombu
5 to 6 cups water

Medium beans – Navy beans, lima beans, black-eyed peas, etc. Soak 4 to 6 hours. Boil 1½ hours. Yield: 4 to 5 cups.

2 cups beans
4-inch piece of kombu
5 to 6 cups water

Small beans – Azuki beans, lentils, split peas, etc. Soak lentils or split peas for 2 to 3 hours. Soak azuki beans 4 to 6 hours. Boil 30 minutes to 1 hour. Yield: 4 to 5 cups.

2 cups beans
4-inch piece of kombu
5 to 6 cups water

Comments – All beans may be boiled until soft. Boiling uses more water and takes more time than pressure cooking. After cooking beans until soft, use one of the procedures for boiled or sauteed dishes as a second step.

Sauteed Bean Dishes

Procedure – Soak beans with kombu and cook until soft, page 81 or 82. Heat oil in another pot and saute onion until transparent. Add vegetables in the order listed, one kind at a time. Saute each kind for 1 to 2 minutes. Add the additional water. Layer beans and bean cooking water on top. Sprinkle salt on top. Cover. Bring to a boil. Simmer 30 to 40 minutes over low heat. Season to taste.

Navy bean soup – Soak beans with kombu for 4 to 6 hours. Boil 1½ hours or pressure cook 30 minutes. Yield: 10 to 12 cups.

2 cups navy beans, boiled
    with a 4-inch piece of kombu
    in 6 cups water (4 cups if pressure cooked)
1 tsp. sesame oil
1 medium onion, minced
2 medium celery stalks, quarter rounds
1 medium carrot, thin quarter rounds
4 or more cups additional water
½ tsp. salt
soy sauce, see seasoning, page 80

Azuki beans with onion – Soak azuki beans with kombu for 4 to 6 hours. Boil for 1 hour. Yield: 5 to 6 cups.

2 cups azuki beans, boiled
    with a 4-inch piece of kombu
    in 5 cups water
½ tsp. sesame oil
1 large onion, minced
¼ tsp. salt
½ cup additional water
soy sauce, see seasoning, page 80

Chickpea spread, hummus – Soak chickpeas with kombu for 6 to 8 hours. Boil for 2 to 2½ hours or pressure cook 45 minutes. After following the basic procedure, puree in a blender with sesame butter, lemon juice, and soy sauce until smooth. Yield: 5 to 6 cups.

---

2 cups chickpeas, boiled
    with a 4-inch piece of kombu
    in 6 cups water (4 cups if pressure cooked)
1 tsp. sesame oil
1 medium onion, minced
2 medium cloves garlic, finely minced
½ cup additional water
½ tsp. salt
2 Tbsp. sesame butter or tahini
1 small lemon, juiced
1 to 2 Tbsp. soy sauce, optional

Lentil soup – Soak lentils with kombu for 2 to 3 hours. Boil 30 to 40 minutes. Yield: 10 to 12 cups.

---

2 cups lentils, boiled
    with a 4-inch piece of kombu
    in 6 cups water
1 tsp. sesame oil
1 medium onion, minced
2 Tbsp. minced parsley
2 medium turnips or rutabagas, diced
2 medium carrots, thin quarter rounds
4 or more cups additional water
½ tsp. salt
soy sauce, see seasoning, page 80

Comments – Cooking beans with oil produces a flavorful dish. It requires two pots; one to cook the beans until soft, and the other to saute the vegetables before adding cooked beans. The beans are not prone to burning because the vegetables are at the bottom of the pot. Other combinations include chickpea, cabbage, carrot, and dumpling soup; kidney bean and roasted cornmeal soup; and azuki bean, onion, sesame butter, and umeboshi paste as a spread.

Sauteed Bean Dishes with Miso

Procedure – Soak beans with kombu and cook until soft, page 81 or 82. Heat oil in another pot and saute onion until transparent. Add vegetables in the order listed, one kind at a time. Saute each kind for 1 to 2 minutes. Add the additional water. Layer beans and cooking water on top. Place miso on top of beans in lumps. Cover. Bring to a boil. Simmer 30 to 40 minutes over low heat.

Pinto bean and tomato miso soup – Soak beans with kombu for 6 to 8 hours. Boil 2 to 2½ hours or pressure cook 45 minutes. Yield: 8 to 10 cups.

---

2 cups pinto beans, boiled
    with a 4-inch piece of kombu
    in 6 cups water (4 cups if pressure cooked)
1 tsp. sesame oil
1 large onion, minced
2 medium tomatoes, diced
1 medium green pepper, diced
4 or more cups additional water
4 to 5 Tbsp. soybean or dark barley miso

Kidney beans with miso – Soak kidney beans with kombu for 6 to 8 hours. Boil 2 to 2½ hours or pressure cook 45 minutes. Yield: 6 to 7 cups.

---

2 cups kidney beans, boiled
    with a 4-inch piece of kombu
    in 6 cups water (4 cups if pressure cooked)
1 tsp. sesame oil
1 large onion, minced
½ cup additional water
4 Tbsp. soybean or dark barley miso

Comments – This procedure is a variation on the basic sauteed bean dish procedure. Instead of using salt and soy sauce, miso is cooked into the beans, making the dish rich and dark.

Sauteed Bean Dishes with Spices

Procedure – Soak beans with kombu and cook until soft, page 81 or 82. Heat oil in another pot and saute onion until transparent. Add vegetables in the order listed, one kind at a time. Saute each kind for 1 to 2 minutes. Add spice. Saute briefly to release flavor and fragrance. Add the additional water. Layer beans and bean cooking water on top. Sprinkle salt on top of the beans. Cover. Bring to a boil. Simmer 30 to 40 minutes over low heat. Season with soy sauce if desired.

Split pea curry sauce – Soak peas with kombu for 2 to 3 hours. Boil for 1 hour. Yield: 6 to 7 cups.

2 cups split peas, boiled
    with a 4-inch piece of kombu
    in 6 cups water
1 tsp. sesame oil
1 large onion, minced
1 large celery stalk, thin quarter rounds
½ tsp. curry powder
1 cup additional water
¼ to ½ tsp. salt
soy sauce, optional; see seasoning, page 80

Pinto beans with chili – Soak beans with kombu for 6 to 8 hours. Boil for 2 to 2½ hours or pressure cook for 45 minutes. Yield: 6 to 7 cups.

---

2 cups pinto beans, boiled
    with a 4-inch piece of kombu
    in 6 cups water (4 cups if pressure cooked)
1 tsp. sesame oil
1 large onion, minced
2 medium garlic cloves, finely minced
½ tsp. chili powder
½ cup additional water
¼ to ½ tsp. salt
soy sauce, optional; see seasoning, page 80

Comments – This procedure is a variation on the basic sauteed bean dish. Spices or herbs are added and sauteed briefly after the last vegetable is sauteed. Sauteing the spice makes it more yang and easier to digest. Also try chickpeas with onion, celery, tomato, and basil.

Boiled Bean Dishes

Procedure – Soak beans with kombu and cook until soft, page 81 or 82. Using the same pot, add the additional water. Mix with beans so water is at the bottom of the pot. Add vegetables. Sprinkle salt on top. Cover. Bring to a boil. Slip a flame tamer under the pot to prevent burning. Simmer 30 to 40 minutes over low heat. Season with soy sauce to taste.

Split pea soup – Soak split peas with kombu for 2 to 3 hours. Boil 1 hour. Yield: 10 to 12 cups.

> 2 cups split peas, boiled
>   with a 4-inch piece of kombu
>   in 6 cups water
> 4 or more cups additional water
> 1 large onion, minced
> 2 large celery stalks, quarter rounds
> 2 medium carrots, thin quarter rounds
> ½ tsp. salt
> soy sauce, see seasoning, page 80

Lima bean soup with noodles – Soak lima beans with kombu for 4 to 6 hours. Boil for 1½ hours or pressure cook for 30 minutes. When cooking soup, add noodles during the last 15 minutes of simmering. Yield: 12 to 14 cups.

> 2 cups lima beans, boiled
>   with a 4-inch piece kombu
>   in 6 cups water (4 cups if pressure cooked)
> 6 or more cups additional water
> 1 medium onion, minced
> 2 Tbsp. minced parsley
> 2 medium ears of corn, cut off the cob
> ½ to ¾ tsp. salt
> 1 cup whole wheat elbow macaroni
> soy sauce, see seasoning, page 80

Azuki beans with winter squash – Soak azuki beans with kombu for 4 to 6 hours. Boil 30 to 45 minutes. Yield: 8 to 10 cups.

---

2 cups azuki beans, cooked
    with a 4-inch piece of kombu
    in 5 cups water
½ cup additional water
1 large butternut squash, 1-inch squares
½ tsp. salt
soy sauce, optional; see seasoning, page 80

Black turtle bean soup – Soak black turtle beans with kombu for 6 to 8 hours. Boil black turtle beans 2 to 2½ hours or pressure cook 45 minutes. Yield: 8 to 10 cups.

---

2 cups black turtle beans, boiled
    with a 4-inch piece of kombu
    in 6 cups water (4 cups water if pressure cooked)
4 or more cups additional water
1 large onion, minced
4 medium yellow squash, quarter rounds
1 medium carrot, shaved
½ tsp. salt
soy sauce, see seasoning, page 80
garnish: scallions, thin rounds, optional

Comments – Making boiled bean dishes involves one utensil. Cook the beans until soft, and then continue to cook the dish in the same pan. If using a pressure cooker, pressure cook the beans, and then boil the dish in the pressure cooker. However, do not lock the cover on the cooker while boiling. Use a different lid, if available. Bean dishes can be simple: after beans are soft, boil with salt or with onion and salt. Dishes can be fancy: after beans are soft, boil with salt, vegetables, grains, noodles, or dumplings, whatever is desired. Other combinations include lentils, barley, and celery; azuki beans, turnips, and carrots; navy beans and millet; and pinto beans, onions, and soy sauce as a spread.

Boiled Bean Dishes with Sesame Butter

Procedure – Soak beans with kombu and cook until soft, page 81 or 82. Using the same pot, add the additional water. Mix with beans so water is at the bottom of the pot. Add vegetables. Sprinkle salt on top. Cover. Bring to a boil. Slip a flame tamer under the pot to prevent burning. Simmer 30 to 40 minutes over low heat. Dilute sesame butter in ½ cup of the hot broth. Add back to dish with soy sauce to heat through but not boil.

> **Chickpea sauce –** Soak chickpeas with kombu for 6 to 8 hours. Boil 2 to 2½ hours or pressure cook 45 minutes. Yield: 10 to 12 cups.

2 cups chickpeas, boiled
   with a 4-inch piece of kombu
   in 6 cups water (4 cups if pressure cooked)
1 cup additional water
1 large celery stalk, thin quarter rounds
1 small cabbage;
   core, finely minced
   leaves, shredded
1 large onion, minced
1 large carrot, quarter rounds
½ tsp. salt
2 to 3 Tbsp. sesame butter
2 to 3 Tbsp. soy sauce

Lentil spread – Soak lentils with kombu for 2 to 3 hours. Boil 30 minutes. If desired, puree spread in blender for smoother texture. Yield: 6 to 7 cups.

---

2 cups lentils, cooked
    with a 4-inch piece of kombu
    in 5 cups water
½ cup additional water
1 medium onion, diced
2 medium celery stalks, thin quarter rounds
¼ tsp. salt
2 Tbsp. sesame butter
1 to 2 Tbsp. soy sauce

Comments – This procedure is a variation on the basic boiled bean dish procedure. The addition of diluted sesame butter makes these dishes creamy. Also try lima beans with onion, celery, and sesame butter.

Pan-Fried Tofu

Procedure – Slice tofu into ½-inch-thick rectangular pieces. Press by placing between two flat surfaces, such as two cutting boards or plates. Set a weight on top, such as a heavy pan or a bottle of water. Let stand 5 minutes. Tilt surfaces to drain. Coat each piece with arrowroot or flour. Heat oil in skillet. Pan-fry tofu until golden, 3 to 4 minutes on each side.

Pan-fried tofu – Yield: 6 to 7 pieces

½ lb. tofu
½ cup arrowroot powder, buckwheat flour,
    or whole wheat flour
1 to 2 Tbsp. corn oil

Comments – Pan-fried tofu is quick to prepare. The tofu is pressed to remove extra water which may cause the oil to splatter when frying. Serve with soy sauce on top, or with scallion miso in a sandwich. It is also good slivered (after frying) and served atop cooked buckwheat noodles.

Tofu Burgers

Procedure – Slice tofu into ¼-inch-thick rectangular pieces. Press by placing between two flat surfaces, such as two cutting boards or plates. Set a weight on top, such as a heavy pan or a bottle of water. Let stand 5 minutes. Tilt surfaces to drain. Mash. Mix with other ingredients. Mixture should hold its shape without being too wet or too dry. Form into patties, 3 to 4 inches in diameter. Heat oil in a skillet. Pan-fry 3 or 4 burgers at a time. Cover skillet for the first side, and fry for 7 minutes. Uncover for the second side, and fry for 5 minutes. Add more oil to skillet for second and third batches.

Tofu burgers – Yield: 8 burgers

½ lb. tofu
½ small onion, finely minced
1 small celery stalk, finely minced
½ small carrot, grated
¼ tsp. salt
½ to ¾ cup whole wheat flour
1 Tbsp. corn oil for skillet

Tofu millet burgers – Yield: 12 burgers

½ lb. tofu
1 cup cooked millet, mashed
1 small onion, finely minced
1 small celery stalk, finely minced
¼ tsp. salt
½ cup whole wheat flour
1 Tbsp. corn oil for skillet

Comments – Tofu burgers make good sandwiches with whole wheat bread or buns and lettuce or pressed cabbage. Also try tofu burgers made with tofu and cooked rice or cooked buckwheat.

Scrambled Tofu

Procedure - Slice tofu into ¼-inch-thick rectangular pieces. Press by placing between two flat surfaces, such as two cutting boards or plates. Set a weight on top, such as a heavy pan or a bottle of water. Let stand 5 minutes. Tilt surfaces to drain. Mash. Heat oil. Add onion and salt. Saute until transparent. Add vegetables in the order listed, one kind at a time. Saute each kind briefly, 1 to 2 minutes. Add tofu (or tofu with millet). Saute 1 to 2 minutes. Cover. Steam 5 minutes over a low flame. Add soy sauce and mix.

Scrambled tofu with vegetables - Yield: 3 to 4 cups.

2 tsp. corn oil
1 small onion, minced
pinch salt
1 cup fresh green peas
1 small carrot, finely minced
½ lb. tofu
1 Tbsp. soy sauce

Scrambled tofu with millet - Mix mashed tofu with cooked millet before adding. Yield: 4 to 5 cups.

2 tsp. corn oil
1 small onion, finely minced
pinch salt
2 small celery stalks, finely minced
½ lb. tofu
½ cup cooked millet
1 Tbsp. soy sauce

Comments - Scrambled tofu resembles scrambled eggs and the two can be combined, page 103. Also try tofu scrambled with cooked rice and scallions, or with onion.

Pan-Fried Tempeh

Procedure – Slice tempeh into thin rectangles and marinate for 5 to 10 minutes or longer. Drain excess liquid and reserve. Heat oil in a skillet. Pan-fry until golden, 2 to 3 minutes for each side. Add reserved marinade and additional water so there is ½ inch of liquid in the pan. Cover pan. Steam 10 to 15 minutes until liquid is gone.

Pan-fried tempeh – Yield: 7 to 8 pieces

> 4 oz. tempeh
> marinade: 2 Tbsp. soy sauce and 2 Tbsp. water, lemon
>   juice, or ginger juice (grate fresh ginger root on a
>   Japanese grater. Squeeze out juice. Discard pulp.)
> 1 Tbsp. corn oil

Comments – Tempeh becomes flavorful when fried in oil. Marinating it first adds more flavor. Pan-fried tempeh makes good sandwiches with whole wheat bread and lettuce or pressed cabbage pickles.

Sauteed Tempeh with Vegetables

Procedure – Cube or crumble tempeh. Marinate 5 to 10 minutes or longer. Drain excess liquid and reserve. Heat oil in pan. Saute onion until transparent. Add vegetables in the order listed, one kind at a time. Saute each kind briefly, 1 to 2 minutes. Add tempeh. Saute for 1 to 2 minutes. Add reserved marinade and additional water so there is ½ inch of liquid in the pan. Cover. Steam 10 to 15 minutes until liquid is gone. Season with more soy sauce if desired.

Tempeh with mushrooms – Yield: 3 to 4 cups.

4 oz. tempeh
marinade: 2 Tbsp. soy sauce and 2 Tbsp. water
2 tsp. corn oil
1 small onion, minced
12 medium mushrooms, thin lengthwise slices
water

Tempeh with red pepper – Yield: 3 to 4 cups.

4 oz. tempeh
marinade: 2 Tbsp. soy sauce and 2 Tbsp. water
2 tsp. corn oil
1 small onion, minced
1 large red bell pepper, diced
water

Comments – Tempeh sauteed with vegetables makes a flavorful side dish. It can also be used as a topping over cooked noodles or raw salad. Try cooking tempeh with onion alone, or with onion and garlic.

Fish and Eggs

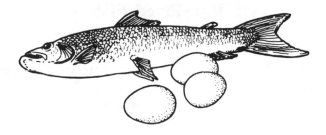

Fish – Wash fish before cooking, especially if storebought and packaged. Rinse quickly under running water to freshen. Pat dry with a paper towel. Fish cooks quickly; it is done when the flesh becomes opaque and begins to flake. Fillets cook faster than whole fish, and thinner pieces cook faster than thicker ones. Since fish continues to cook after being removed from the heat, you should undercook it slightly. Overcooked fish can be tough.

Fish is high in sodium so it is often balanced by marinating in ginger juice or lemon juice, or by serving with lemon slices, grated daikon radish, or with salad. Use freshly grated ginger juice. Grate fresh ginger with a Japanese grater. Squeeze out juice. Discard pulp.

Soy sauce or salt used in preparing fish helps remove the fish odor and helps keep the fish tender as it cooks.

Eggs – Eggs cook quickly. In baking, eggs are cooked for the full time into a dish; but in soups or fried dishes, eggs are added at the end of cooking. Eggs can be cooked with quick cooking foods, such as sprouts, or with lightly cooked foods, such as sauteed onions. Eggs are high in sodium, so they are often balanced by cooking or serving with sprouts, green peppers, or oranges.

Pan-Fried Fish

Procedure – Rinse and dry fish and cut into serving-sized pieces. Pour marinade over fish. Let stand 5 minutes. Turn fish over and let stand another 5 minutes. Remove from marinade. Cover with coating. Heat oil in a skillet. Fry fish 2 to 3 minutes, covered. Turn and fry the second side without a cover for 2 to 3 minutes or until browned.

Pan-fried perch

1 to 2 lbs. perch fillets or other fresh fish
marinade: 1 Tbsp. equal parts soy sauce and freshly
    squeezed lemon juice or freshly grated ginger juice
    per 4 oz. of fish
coating: arrowroot flour, fine cornmeal, or whole wheat
    pastry flour
1 Tbsp. corn oil for skillet

Comments – For pan-frying, it is best to use fillets, but whole fish can be pan-fried, too. Slit whole fish down the backbone and open to marinate. Allow more time for frying. Fish is done when the flesh begins to flake. Serve with lemon slices and/or salad; or add to Kombu Soup with Vegetables, page 67.

Broiled Fish

Procedure – Rinse and dry fish. For fillets, cut into serving-sized pieces. For whole fish, slit down backbone and open. Pour marinade over fish. Let stand 5 minutes. Turn fish over and let stand another 5 minutes. Remove from marinade and place on oiled broiling pan. Place under broiler and watch carefully. Thicker fish should be turned once. Remove when flesh begins to flake.

Broiled salmon

> 1 to 2 lbs. salmon or other fresh fish
> marinade: 1 Tbsp. equal parts soy sauce and freshly
>   squeezed lemon juice or freshly grated ginger juice
>   per 4 oz. of fish

Comments – Broiling uses heat as high as 500 to 600 degrees. Food is placed under the heat so it is cooked from above. The closer the fish is to the heat, the faster it will cook. Thin fillets can broil in 3 to 4 minutes if close to the heat, but may require up to 8 minutes if further from the heat. Since the size and kind of fish and ovens vary, watch carefully. Remove immediately when the flesh begins to flake. If desired, sprinkle herbs such as basil or sage on top before broiling. You can also brush marinade on the fish once or twice during broiling so fish is more tender and flavorful.

Baked Fish

Procedure – Rinse and dry fish. For fillets, cut into serving-sized pieces. For whole fish, slit down backbone and open. Pour marinade over fish. Let stand 5 minutes. Turn fish over and let stand another 5 minutes. Place fish and marinade in baking dish. Bake at 350 degrees until flesh begins to flake.

Baked trout

---
2 trout, whole, or other fresh fish
marinade: 1 Tbsp. equal parts soy sauce and freshly
    squeezed lemon juice or freshly grated ginger juice
    per 4 oz. of fish

Comments – Any fish can be baked, with good results. Whole fish and thicker pieces of fish need to be baked longer. Thin fillets can bake in 10 minutes, while thick ones may take 20 minutes. If desired, cover the dish to keep the fish moist.

Baked Fish with Vegetables

Procedure – Rinse and dry fish. Slit whole fish down backbone and open. Pour marinade over fish and let stand 5 minutes. Turn fish over and let stand another 5 minutes. Saute vegetables in oil until half done, 10 to 15 minutes. Place fish, marinade, and vegetables in oiled casserole dish. Add water if needed so ¼-inch of liquid is at bottom. Cover dish. Bake 25 to 30 minutes at 350 degrees, until flesh begins to flake.

Baked fish with onion

½ to 1 lb. whole fish
marinade: 1 Tbsp. equal parts soy sauce and freshly
    squeezed lemon juice or freshly grated ginger juice
    per 4 oz. of fish
1 tsp. sesame oil
1 large onion, minced
boiling water as needed

Baked fish with carrots and potatoes – Saute vegetables by adding in the order listed.

½ to 1 lb. whole fish
marinade: 1 Tbsp. equal parts soy sauce and freshly
    squeezed lemon juice or freshly grated ginger juice
    per 4 oz. of fish
1 tsp. sesame oil
1 large onion, minced
3 medium potatoes, diced
2 small carrots, shaved
boiling water as needed

Comments – Baking is a good method to cook whole fish. The cover keeps the fish and vegetables moist. Also try yellow squash, green peppers, or fresh mushrooms.

Steamed Fish

Procedure – Rinse and dry fish. Add water to the pan to a depth of ¼ inch. Bring to a boil. Add salt. Add fish and sprinkle herbs on top. Cover. Steam fish 3 to 4 minutes until flesh begins to flake.

Steamed cod

1 to 2 lbs. cod fillets or other fresh fish
boiling water as needed
pinch salt
½ to 1 tsp. basil

Comments – For steaming it is best to use fillets. It produces light fish, making a nice summertime fish dish. Fish steam quickly; don't overcook, as fish can become tough. Try adding 1 Tbsp. lemon juice to the boiling water or steaming fish with parsley.

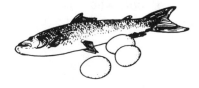

Scrambled Eggs

Procedure – Beat eggs. Add other ingredients. Mix well. Heat oil in a skillet. Add mixture. Fry over medium heat, stirring constantly until the eggs are cooked through and are a dull yellow, 3 to 4 minutes. For mixture with tofu, cover pan and steam an additional 2 to 3 minutes.

Scrambled eggs

2 eggs
2 Tbsp. lemon or orange juice, freshly squeezed
pinch salt or ¼ tsp. soy sauce
2 tsp. corn oil for skillet

Scrambled egg with tofu

1 egg
½ lb. tofu, pressed and mashed, page 94
1 Tbsp. lemon or orange juice, freshly squeezed
⅛ tsp. salt, or ½ tsp. soy sauce
2 tsp. corn oil for skillet

Scrambled egg with millet

1 egg
1 cup cooked and cooled millet, mashed
4 medium scallions, thin rounds
1 Tbsp. lemon or orange juice, freshly squeezed
pinch salt or ¼ tsp. soy sauce
2 tsp. corn oil for skillet

Comments – Scrambled eggs are enhanced by adding citrus juice and soy sauce. Also try adding cooked rice, chopped sprouts, or mixing tofu, millet, and egg together.

Scrambled Eggs with Cooked Vegetables

Procedure – Heat oil in a skillet. Saute onion until transparent. Add vegetables. Saute for 1 to 2 minutes. Add water, tofu and/or grain if used, and salt. Cover. Steam 5 to 7 minutes until water is gone. Add egg. Scramble until egg is cooked, 3 to 4 minutes.

Scrambled egg with red pepper and tofu

2 tsp. corn oil
1 large onion, minced
1 large red bell pepper, diced
¼ cup water
½ lb. tofu, pressed and mashed, page 94
pinch salt
1 egg, beaten

Scrambled egg with rice and celery

2 tsp. corn oil
1 large onion, minced
1 large celery stalk, diced
¼ cup water
1 cup cooked brown rice
pinch salt
1 egg, beaten

Comments – This procedure uses finely cut vegetables. Try eggs with vegetables alone, such as onion and egg, or onion, egg, and broccoli. Also try mixing tofu, grain, and egg together.

Salads
and
Dressings

Vegetables – Use young fresh vegetables for a tender and crisp salad. Wash vegetables well and dry completely. Pat dry with a towel if necessary.

Dressings – Salad dressings can be thick or thin depending on choice of salad. Generally, thinner dressings are mixed with raw or medley salads or served separately. Thicker dressings are mixed with cooked salads or used as dips. Make dressings in small amounts for use at one meal. If boiled, sauteed, or heated, let dressing cool before mixing or serving with salad.

Other salads – The recipes in this section are only a sample of the many different salads you can make. Use other dressings or add other vegetables to create your own salads. Other salad recipes can be found under Pickles and Pressed Salads, and Sea Vegetables.

Cooked Salads, Whole Vegetables

Procedure – Bring water to a boil in a large pan over medium to medium-high heat. Add salt. Cook vegetables in the order listed, one kind at a time. For broccoli and cauliflower, stand upright, stem closest to bottom of pan. Bring to a boil without covering pan. Boil briefly, until a toothpick can be inserted, 4 to 5 minutes, or longer if pieces are especially thick. For broccoli and cauliflower, turn and boil flower side down another 30 seconds. Remove. Drain in colander. Separate pieces so they cool. Repeat with each kind of vegetable. Cool completely. Cut. Gently mix with dressing, add toppings, or serve as dipping vegetables.

Green bean salad with almonds – Yield: 4 to 5 cups.

    4 cups water
    ⅛ tsp. salt
    20 to 25 medium green beans, whole; cut into
        2-inch lengths when cool
    dressing: Nut butter dressing (use almond butter,
        soy sauce, and water), page 115;
    or, topping: Roasted almonds (½ cup) with soy sauce,
        page 127

Salad vegetables and dips – Yield: 8 to 10 cups.

    6 cups water
    ¼ tsp. salt
    1 small bunch broccoli; cut each stalk 3 inches below
        flower (retain bottom stem for another use);
        separate into flowerettes after cooking
    1 small cauliflower; leave whole but remove bottom stem;
        separate into flowerettes after cooking
    3 medium carrots, halved; cut into logs or 1-inch rounds
        after cooking
    dipping sauce: Tofu and sesame butter sauce, page 125;
        or, Walnut sauce with soy sauce, page 123;
        or, Nut butter and soy sauce gravy (use sesame butter
            and omit scallions), page 122

Comments – By cooked salad I mean a style of cooking that uses salted boiling water and no cover. This book includes three procedures for preparing cooked salads (whole, cut, and leafy vegetables). Vegetables boiled without a cover keep their bright color. Although cut vegetables cook faster, whole vegetables retain more flavor. By removing them when the water returns to a boil, vegetables stay crisp. Choose thick dressings; they will be thinned by the boiled vegetables. Save the cooking water to make soup; just season with soy sauce or cook vegetables in it.

A cooked salad can be used as a salad or as a vegetable dish depending on how tender or crisp the vegetables are cooked. I like to experiment, using different ingredients or combining methods. Try cooked green beans or yellow squash on a raw lettuce salad, cooked leafy greens of kale or endive sprinkled with roasted seeds or nuts, or parsnips or celery cooked whole and then cut for use with dips.

Cooked Salads, Cut Vegetables

Procedure – Bring water to a boil in a large pan over medium to medium-high heat. Add salt. Cook vegetables in the order listed, one kind at a time. Bring to a boil without covering pan. Remove vegetables when water returns to a rolling boil. Drain in colander. Spread thinly to cool. Repeat with each kind of vegetable. Cool completely. Gently mix all vegetables with dressing.

Lettuce cooked salad – Yield: 4 cups.

> 4 cups water
> ⅛ tsp. salt
> 1 medium lettuce (iceberg, romaine, butter, leaf), shredded
> dressing: Umeboshi dressing (use lemon juice and
>   omit butter), page 115.

Cabbage, carrot, and celery cooked salad – Yield: 6 to 7 cups.

> 6 cups water
> ¼ tsp. salt
> 1 small cabbage (core removed), shredded
> 2 medium celery stalks, thin diagonals
> 1 medium carrot, thin matchsticks
> dressing: Soy sauce dressing (use lemon juice), page 115;
>   or, Umeboshi and scallion dressing (use 3 plums),
>   page 117;
>   or, Onion and lemon dressing, page 116

Comments – See comments under Cooked Salads, Whole Vegetables, page 107.

Cooked Salads, Leafy Vegetables

Procedure – Bring water to a boil in a large pan over medium to medium-high heat. Add salt. Cook vegetables in the order listed, one kind at a time. Stand up greens in pan, so that the stems or hard parts are standing on the bottom. Bring to a boil without covering the pan. Immerse leafy parts when stems wilt, after about 1 minute of boiling. Boil leaves briefly, 1 to 2 minutes, or longer if thick. Remove. Drain in a colander. Lay each leaf separately over the edge to cool. Repeat with each kind of vegetable. When cool, squeeze gently to remove excess water. Cut into 1-inch pieces. Gently mix all vegetables with dressing.

Mustard greens cooked salad – Yield: 4 cups.

4 cups water
⅛ tsp. salt
1 medium bunch mustard greens, whole leaves
dressing: 2 to 3 Tbsp. Sesame salt, page 129.

Spinach and cabbage cooked salad – Yield: 5 to 6 cups.

6 cups water
¼ tsp. salt
1 bunch spinach, whole leaves
8 medium leaves Chinese cabbage, whole and separated
    from head
dressing: Nut butter dressing (use sesame butter, soy
    sauce, and water), page 115

Comments – See comments under Cooked Salads, Whole Vegetables, page 107.

Medley Salads

Procedure – Mix dressing. Gently mix ingredients into dressing in the order listed, one kind at a time. Allow flavors to mingle for 30 minutes to 1 hour before serving.

Rice salad – Yield: 6 to 7 cups.

dressing: Onion and soy sauce dressing (add more soy
    sauce if desired), page 116
½ small carrot, grated
1 medium cucumber, thin quarter rounds
1 small (or ½ medium) lettuce, torn into bite-sized squares
2 cups cooked brown rice, cooled, page 7 or 10

Bulghur salad – Yield: 6 to 7 cups.

dressing: Oil and lemon dressing, page 118
½ cup chopped parsley
4 medium scallions, thin rounds
2 medium celery stalks, thin quarter rounds
4 large radishes, half rounds
3 cups cooked bulghur, cooled, page 12

Noodle salad – Yield: 6 to 7 cups.

dressing: Tofu and umeboshi sauce, page 125
2 small celery stalks, thin quarter rounds
1 medium red bell pepper, diced
1 small (or ½ medium) lettuce, torn into bite-sized squares
2 cups cooked whole wheat elbow macaroni, cooled,
    page 23

Rice and corn salad - Yield 6 to 7 cups

dressing: Umeboshi and scallion dressing (use 3 plums),
    page 117
1 small cucumber, thin quarter rounds
2 medium ears of corn, cooked and cut off of the cob
1 small (or ½ medium) lettuce, torn into bite-sized squares
2 cups cooked brown rice, cooled, page 7 or 10

Comments - Medley salads are a nice way to prepare a whole meal in one dish, especially in the summer. For more flavor, use more seasoning in the dressing. Try other salads; rice, lettuce, celery, and cucumbers with boiled umeboshi dressing; or whole wheat shells, lettuce, and scallions with heated oil and vinegar dressing.

Raw Salads, Tossed

Procedure – Gently combine salad ingredients. Mix dressing and serve separately.

> **Tossed salad –** Combine 3 or 4 of the following ingredients.
>
> ---
>
> lettuce, torn into bite-sized squares
> cucumber, thin rounds, half-rounds, or quarter-rounds
> radish, thin rounds or half-rounds
> small celery stalks, thin quarter rounds
> carrot, grated
> scallion, thin rounds
> sprouts, whole
> red bell pepper, diced or thin crescents
> avocado, chunks
> zucchini or yellow squash, young ones, thin rounds or
>   half-rounds
>
> ---

Comments – Raw salad is easy to prepare for a hot summer day or as part of an elaborate meal. Use a simple, mixed dressing, thinning so it is pourable, page 115.

Raw Salads, Layered

Procedure – Layer ingredients in the order listed. Mix dressing and serve separately.

Lettuce, cucumber, and sunflower salad – Yield: 4 to 5 cups.

½ medium lettuce, torn into bite-sized squares
½ small carrot, grated
1 medium cucumber, half-rounds
roasted sunflower seeds, page 127
dressing: Soy sauce dressing (use lemon juice), page 115

Lettuce, radish, and avocado salad – Yield: 4 to 5 cups.

½ medium lettuce, torn into bite-sized squares
4 large radishes, thin rounds
2 medium scallions, thin rounds
1 avocado, chunks
dressing: Umeboshi dressing (use lime juice and omit
    nut butter), page 115

Comments – Layered salads are good arranged in individual bowls. Different colors make attractive salads. Serve with a simple, pourable dressing.

Raw Salads, Tossed with Dressing

Procedure – Make dressing. Cool for 5 minutes if dressing was cooked. Gently mix salad ingredients into the dressing in the order listed, one kind at a time. Let salad stand 10 minutes before serving to allow flavors to mingle.

Lettuce, carrot, and sprouts salad – Yield: 6 to 7 cups.

dressing: Onion and soy sauce dressing (use brown rice
    vinegar), page 116
½ cup alfalfa sprouts
1 small carrot, grated
1 medium (or ½ large) lettuce, torn into bite-sized squares

Cucumber and avocado salad – Yield: 4 to 5 cups.

dressing: Avocado dressing, page 115
2 medium scallions, thin rounds
2 small celery stalks, thin quarter rounds
2 large cucumbers, thin quarter rounds

Lettuce and tofu salad – Yield: 6 to 7 cups.

dressing: Tofu and sesame butter sauce (use soy sauce
    and water), page 125
2 medium scallions, thin rounds
4 medium radishes, thin rounds
3 small celery stalks, thin quarter rounds
1 medium (or ½ large) lettuce, torn into bite-sized squares

Comments – Tossing the salad with the dressing is preferable when the dressing is thick and not easily poured or when the dressing is boiled or sauteed. Try boiled umeboshi dressing with radishes and lettuce; or heated oil and vinegar dressing with lettuce, cucumbers, and young, tender yellow squash.

Salad Dressings, Mixed

Procedure – Mix ingredients together. Cream butters, umeboshi, or miso with each other first. Then add liquid. Thin until pourable or to desired consistency. Gently toss with salad or serve separately.

Soy sauce dressing – for 4 to 6 cups vegetables. Yield: ¼ cup.

2 Tbsp. soy sauce
2 Tbsp. lemon juice or brown rice vinegar

Umeboshi dressing – for 4 to 6 cups vegetables. Yield: ¼ cup.

1 Tbsp. umeboshi paste
1 Tbsp. nut or seed butter; optional
water, lemon, or lime juice for thinning

Nut butter dressing – for 4 to 6 cups vegetables. Yield: ¼ cup.

1 Tbsp. nut or seed butter
1 Tbsp. light miso or soy sauce
water, lemon, or orange juice for thinning

Avocado dressing – for 4 to 6 cups vegetables. Yield: 1 cup.

1 large avocado, pitted and mashed
½ large lemon, juiced
soy sauce to equal amount of juice

Comments – Mixed dressings are fast to make. They can be thin or thick, depending on choice of salad. Make thinner when dressing will be served separately. Use fresh, soft ingredients.

Salad Dressings, Sauteed

Procedure – Heat oil. Saute onion with salt, if used, until transparent. Cover pan. Saute 5 more minutes over low heat. Remove from heat. Cool 5 minutes. Mix with other dressing ingredients. Let stand 10 minutes. Gently mix with salad.

Onion and lemon dressing – for 4 to 6 cups vegetables. Yield: 1 cup.

> 1 Tbsp. sesame oil
> 1 small onion, finely minced
> ½ tsp. salt
> 1 small lemon, juiced

Onion and umeboshi dressing – for 4 to 6 cups vegetables. Yield: 1 cup.

> 1 Tbsp. sesame oil
> 1 small onion, finely minced
> 1 Tbsp. umeboshi paste
> water or lemon juice for thinning

Onion and soy sauce dressing – for 4 to 6 cups vegetables. Yield: 1 cup.

> 1 Tbsp. sesame oil
> 1 small onion, finely minced
> 1 to 2 Tbsp. soy sauce
> 1 Tbsp. brown rice vinegar; optional

Comments – Sauteed dressings use onions, which add much flavor to a salad. They are best when cooled before mixing with the salad. Allow to stand 10 to 15 minutes before serving to let flavors mingle.

Salad Dressings, Boiled

Procedure – Boil umeboshi plums in the water until soft, 5 to 10 minutes. Remove pits. Mash plums with the cooking water and the other ingredients, using a blender or suribachi. Gently mix with salad.

Umeboshi and scallion dressing – for 8 to 10 cups vegetables. Yield: ½ cup.

4 medium umeboshi plums, whole
¼ cup water
2 medium scallions, thin rounds

Umeboshi and nut butter dressing – for 8 to 10 cups vegetables. Yield: ½ cup.

4 medium umeboshi plums, whole
¼ cup water
1 Tbsp. nut or seed butter
1 small lemon, juiced

Comments – These dressings are boiled because they use whole umeboshi plums, which need to be softened before pitting and blending. Sauteed onions make a nice addition.

Salad Dressings, Heated

Procedure – Heat oil until hot, 4 to 5 minutes. Cool completely, 10 to 12 minutes. Mix well with other ingredients. Gently mix into dish.

Oil and soy sauce dressing – for 6 to 8 cups vegetables. Yield: ¼ cup.

1 Tbsp. sesame oil
3 to 4 Tbsp. soy sauce

Oil and vinegar dressing – for 6 to 8 cups vegetables. Yield: ¼ cup.

1 Tbsp. sesame oil
½ tsp. salt
3 Tbsp. brown rice vinegar

Oil and lemon dressing – for 6 to 8 cups vegetables. Yield: ¼ cup.

1 Tbsp. sesame oil
½ tsp. salt
1 large lemon, juiced

Comments – Heating oil before making a dressing increases its flavor. The oil and soy sauce dressing also makes a good sauce for cooked vegetables. It complements cooked spaghetti squash well. Mix heated dressings with the dish as they tend to separate if allowed to stand.

Sauces and Condiments

Mixed Sauces

Procedure – Grate fresh ginger root on a Japanese grater. Squeeze out juice. Discard pulp. Mix with other ingredients.

Soy and ginger sauce – Yield: about ¼ cup.

1 Tbsp. fresh ginger juice
3 to 4 Tbsp. soy sauce

Soy and ginger dipping sauce – Yield: ¼ to ½ cup.

1 Tbsp. fresh ginger juice
3 to 4 Tbsp. soy sauce
1 to 2 Tbsp. boiling water

Comments – Mixing soy sauce with ginger makes a versatile sauce which complements fried foods well, such as fish, burgers, or pancakes. It can be used as a marinade for tempeh or fish. The dipping sauce is good with raw vegetables, cooked salads, or over noodles.

Clear Sauces

Procedure – Heat oil. Saute onion until transparent. Add half of the water listed. Cover. Bring to a boil. Simmer 5 minutes over low heat. Dissolve arrowroot or kuzu in the other half of the cold water. Add to pan. Simmer until thick and clear, 1 to 2 minutes, stirring constantly. Add soy sauce.

Thick clear sauce – Yield: 2 cups.

1 Tbsp. sesame oil
1 medium onion, finely minced
2 cups cold water
2 Tbsp. arrowroot or kuzu
2 Tbsp. soy sauce

Medium clear sauce – Yield: 2 cups.

1 Tbsp. sesame oil
1 medium onion, finely minced
2 cups cold water
4 tsp. arrowroot or kuzu
2 Tbsp. soy sauce

Thin clear sauce (like a broth) – Yield: 2 cups.

1 Tbsp. sesame oil
1 medium onion, finely minced
2 cups cold water
2 tsp. arrowroot or kuzu
2 Tbsp. soy sauce

Comments – Serve clear sauces with grains and noodles. Make in small amounts for use at one meal and make 10 to 15 minutes before serving. For variety, try cooking herbs into the sauce, such as ¼ tsp. basil or parsley. Or, saute 1 clove of finely minced garlic with the onion.

Bechamel Sauces

Procedure – Heat oil. Add flour. Saute until fragrant, 1 to 2 minutes. Stir constantly to smooth lumps. Remove from heat. Cool completely, 10 to 15 minutes. Mix in one half the amount of cold water listed. Place over medium heat. Slowly add the rest of the cold water, stirring constantly. Use a wire whisk if necessary to smooth lumps. Add salt. Cover. Bring to a boil. Simmer 20 to 25 minutes over low heat. Stir occasionally. Add water if needed to maintain desired consistency.

Basic bechamel sauce – Yield: 2 cups.

1 to 2 Tbsp. sesame oil
4 Tbsp. whole wheat pastry flour
1 to 2 cups cold water
¼ tsp. salt

Comments – Many different sauces can be made from this general recipe. Basically, bechamel sauce is made by sauteing the flour in oil and then simmering with water and salt. You can use as little as ½ teaspoon oil. More oil makes a richer and more flavorful sauce. Saute the flour longer to make a darker sauce. Simmer longer or without a cover to make a thicker sauce, or add more water to make a thinner sauce.

Use different flours for variety. Try brown rice flour or sweet brown rice flour for a lighter sauce, or whole wheat flour for a heavier sauce. Corn flour, buckwheat flour, or rye flour can be used also. Use different oils for various flavors, such as sunflower oil or corn oil. Also try simmering with herbs, such as ¼ teaspoon parsley, chives, or basil; or seasoning to taste with soy sauce or diluted miso at the end of cooking.

Serve bechamel sauces over cooked vegetables, noodles, or grains, adding a garnish on top if desired, such as thin rounds of scallions or fresh parsley. Bechamel sauces can be mixed into casseroles or vegetable pie fillings.

Nut Butter Sauces

Procedure – Cream nut or seed butter with miso or soy sauce, then cream with ¼ cup water. Add scallions, if used. Place over medium heat and add the rest of the water gradually, until thinned to the desired consistency. Heat until it boils, 3 to 4 minutes, stirring constantly. It will thicken, so add more water or other liquid if needed to maintain desired consistency.

Nut butter and soy sauce gravy – Yield: 1 to 1½ cups.

3 Tbsp. nut or seed butter
1 Tbsp. soy sauce
¾ to 1 cup water
4 medium scallions, thin rounds; optional

Nut butter and miso gravy – Yield: 1 to 1½ cups.

3 Tbsp. nut or seed butter
1 Tbsp. miso
¾ to 1 cup water
4 medium scallions, thin rounds; optional

Comments – Nut butter sauces are rich and flavorful. They can be made quickly and are best when served hot. When serving over noodles or vegetables, make a thin sauce or else it will be too rich. Use thick sauce as a dip or spread.

Vary sauces by using different nut or seed butters. Sesame butter or tahini produces a sauce complementary to most grains, while almond or peanut butter produces a rich sauce which better complements simmered vegetables or cooked salads. Try adding other liquids for flavor. After sauce boils and thickens, remove from heat and add 1 Tbsp. brown rice vinegar, or lemon, lime, or orange juice. Peanut butter, miso, and orange juice make a tangy sauce.

Chunky Sauces

Procedure – Roast nuts or seeds by the top-of-the-stove method, page 127. Chop with a knife if nuts are large or firm. Grind in a blender or suribachi until three-fourths of the nuts or seeds are crushed. Add miso or soy sauce. Grind together. Add water until creamy and thinned to desired consistency.

Walnut sauce with miso – Yield: 1 cup.

1 cup walnuts
1 Tbsp. dark miso
boiling water for thinning

Walnut sauce with soy sauce – Yield: 1 cup.

1 cup walnuts
1 Tbsp. soy sauce
boiling water for thinning

Peanut sauce with miso – Yield: 1 cup.

1 cup peanuts
1 Tbsp. dark miso
boiling water for thinning

Comments – Sauces made with freshly ground nuts taste fresher than sauces made with nut or seed butters. Make thick and use as a spread, or make thin and use as a sauce over noodles or grain. Walnuts grind easily and make a good sauce over rice. Also try almonds or sesame seeds. A dark miso such as soybean or 2-year-old barley produces a delicious sauce. For more information on using a suribachi, see page 243.

Miso Sauces

Procedure – Heat oil. Add miso. Saute until fragrant, 1 to 2 minutes, stirring constantly to smooth lumps. Add liquid gradually, thinning to desired consistency. For thin sauce, bring to a boil after adding liquid.

Thick miso sauce – Yield: ¼ cup.

1 Tbsp. sesame oil
3 Tbsp. dark miso
2 to 4 Tbsp. water, lemon, or orange juice

Thin miso sauce – Yield: 1¼ cup.

1 Tbsp. sesame oil
3 Tbsp. dark miso
¾ to 1 cup water

Comments – Miso sauces are flavorful. The oil and miso complement each other. A dark miso such as soybean or 2-year-old barley produces a delicious sauce, yet lighter or younger miso also can be used. The thick sauce can be used as a spread; the thin sauce can be used as a dip. Both are good with raw or simmered vegetables. For variety, add thin rounds of scallions.

Tofu Sauces

Procedure – Boil tofu in water until puffy, about 5 minutes. Drain and discard water. Blend with other ingredients in a blender until smooth, thinning to desired consistency.

Tofu and sesame butter sauce – Yield: 1 to 2 cups.

½ lb. tofu, 1-inch cubes
½ cup water
1 to 2 Tbsp. sesame butter or tahini
2 Tbsp. soy sauce or 1 Tbsp. miso
water or lemon juice for thinning

Tofu and umeboshi sauce – Use soft umeboshi plums and puree in blender before adding tofu. Yield: 1 to 2 cups.

½ lb. tofu, 1-inch cubes
½ cup water
4 medium umeboshi plums, pitted
1 to 2 tsp. sesame oil, heated and cooled
water or lemon juice for thinning

Comments – Tofu sauces can be used as spreads, dressings, sauces, or mixed into dishes. Make sauce thicker and use as a dip or spread; make thinner and use as a topping or an ingredient in a dish. The tofu is boiled to make it more digestible and the oil is heated to give better flavor. For variation, saute 1 clove of finely minced garlic in the oil before blending, or gently mix thin rounds of scallions or chopped alfalfa sprouts into the blended sauce.

Roasted Nuts and Seeds, Oven

Procedure – Place one layer of any kind of nut or seed on a baking sheet. Place in a pre-heated, 350-degree oven. Roast until fragrant, beginning to pop, and browning. Stir occasionally.

almonds, 15 to 20 minutes
peanuts, 25 to 30 minutes
cashews, 10 to 12 minutes
walnuts, 10 to 12 minutes
pumpkin seeds, 10 to 12 minutes
sunflower seeds, 10 to 15 minutes

Comments – Roasting nuts or seeds in an oven is a good method for roasting a larger quantity. However, it is harder to control the temperature in an oven, and seeds or nuts may not roast uniformly. For mixed roasted nuts, roast separately, even if both take the same time. If roasted together, they may not roast uniformly or completely. After roasting, they can be mixed while still warm.

Try adding soy sauce after roasting. Place hot roasted nuts or seeds in a bowl. Add 3 or 4 drops soy sauce per ¼ cup seeds or nuts. They will sizzle. Stir to coat. Try not to add too much soy sauce as nuts and seeds can get soggy. If this happens, return to oven to dry out.

Enjoy roasted nuts or seeds as a snack, as a crunchy topping for noodles, grains, or cooked vegetables, or in baked goods. Be careful not to eat too many as they can be quite rich.

Roasted Nuts and Seeds, Top of Stove

Procedure – Place a quarter-inch layer of any kind of seed or nut in a skillet. Dry roast (no oil) over medium heat until fragrant, beginning to pop, and browning. Stir often or shake every 30 seconds. Remove from heat and let stand in the hot pan a few extra minutes to complete roasting.

almonds, 7 to 10 minutes
peanuts, 10 to 15 minutes
cashews, 5 to 7 minutes
walnuts, 5 to 7 minutes
pumpkin seeds, 5 to 7 minutes
sunflower seeds, 5 to 7 minutes
sesame seeds (wash and drain before roasting),
    5 to 7 minutes

Comments – Roasting nuts or seeds on top of the stove is quick and a good method to use when roasting a small amount. Because they have closer contact with the heat and are stirred often when in a skillet, they roast more uniformly than in the oven. Nuts and seeds are done when they have changed flavor throughout; they don't have to be completely browned. By allowing them to remain in the pan for extra time, they will receive the heat of the pan to complete roasting the insides without over-browning the outsides. Let larger nuts remain in the pan longer than smaller seeds. If the pan is already hot, roasting may be faster than the times specified.

Try adding soy sauce after roasting. Place hot nuts or seeds in a bowl. Add 3 or 4 drops of soy sauce per ¼ cup nuts or seeds. They will sizzle. Stir to coat. Try not to add too much soy sauce or nuts or seeds can become soggy. If this happens, return to pan to dry out.

Roasted Sesame Seeds, Covered Skillet

Procedure – Wash seeds. Drain until dry, 3 to 4 hours. Place one very thin layer of seeds, 1 to 2 Tbsp., in a lightweight, dry skillet (no oil). Cover. Roast over medium heat. Shake pan every 5 to 10 seconds. Seeds will pop, smell fragrant, and brown. They will be easy to crush between two fingers. Remove to bowl and continue for all seeds. The first layer will roast in about 2 minutes; later batches will roast quicker as the pan becomes hotter.

Roasted sesame seeds

1 cup sesame seeds

Comments – Roasting small amounts in a covered skillet is a thorough way to roast sesame seeds. The seeds have more contact with the heat than when they are roasted in large amounts. The cover keeps the popping seeds and the heat inside. This is the preferred way to roast seeds that will be used in condiments (page 129). If the seeds will be added to dough, they can be roasted by the top-of-the-stove method, as they will roast again when baked. Each method takes the same amount of time overall to roast the same quantity of seeds; one cup of seeds will take about 15 minutes to roast by either method.

If you don't have time to air dry the washed seeds for 3 to 4 hours, place all seeds in a dry skillet (no oil) and stir seeds until all water is evaporated. Then remove and roast in small amounts.

Roasted Sesame Seed Condiments

Procedure – Place salt, if used, in a dry skillet (no oil) and roast over medium heat for one minute, stirring constantly. Roast wakame if used, page 78. Place hot wakame or salt in suribachi. Grind to a fine powder. Roast sesame seeds by the covered skillet method, page 128. Add to suribachi and grind gently until three-fourths of the seeds are crushed.

Sesame seed salt (gomashio) – Yield: 1 cup.

1 Tbsp. salt
1 cup sesame seeds

Sesame seed and wakame condiment – Yield: 1 cup.

3 strips wakame, will make about 2 Tbsp. powder
1 cup sesame seeds

Comments – To make sesame seed condiments, a suribachi is necessary, page 243. Roasting the salt before making gomashio dries the salt and makes it easier to grind. These condiments will keep for up to 1 month. For variety, change the proportions to make a more or less salty condiment.

Sesame seed condiments are a good complement to grains, noodles, vegetables, cooked salads, or almost any dish.

Spreads

Procedure – Cream ingredients together. Add liquid if needed to thin to spreadable consistency.

Nut butter and miso spread – Yield: ½ cup.

¼ cup nut or seed butter
1 to 2 tsp. miso
water for thinning

Nut butter and soy sauce spread – Yield: ½ cup.

¼ cup nut or seed butter
2 to 3 tsp. soy sauce
water for thinning

Comments – These basic nut butter spreads can be made with sesame butter, tahini, peanut butter, almond butter, etc. Try adding thin rounds of scallions or chopped alfalfa sprouts for variety. Other spreads can be made from thick nut butter sauces, chunky sauces, miso sauces, or tofu sauces. Blended beans also make good spreads.

Pickles
and
Pressed Salads

Fermentation – Pickles are a fermented food. Fermentation is a process of breaking down the food so it is digestible. Bacteria aid in the fermentation and provide enzymes and vitamins which are beneficial to the body. When making pickles in brine, bubbles will rise, which signal that there is good fermentation.

Natural pickling all year around – Pickles can be made in any season. Small batches are made and eaten; when the supply is low, more are made. Vegetables are pickled by the action of bacteria and salt. Vinegar, canning, and boiling are not used as each can destroy beneficial bacteria. Pickle at room temperature. In summer, pickling is faster because bacteria are more active.

Duration of pickling – Pickling can be done in a short time, 1 to 2 hours, as in quick pressed salads; or in a long time, 2 weeks, as in sauerkraut. Generally, pickles are done when they change color and flavor, and the salt has permeated them. Pressed salads are done when they have condensed and absorbed some salt but are still crisp.

Vegetables – Use clean, blemish-free vegetables. Young crisp vegetables make better pickles than old tough vegetables. Wash and dry vegetables before starting pickles. Vegetables that are at room temperature produce better pickles than vegetables right out of the refrigerator, so let vegetables stand at room temperature 1 hour before pickling.

Salt – Salt keeps the bacteria in check. It permeates the vegetables, adding flavor and preserving them. Salt also makes the pickles alkaline-forming so they complement acid-forming grains. For pickles made in bran or brine, the longer the pickles stay in the medium, the more salty they become.

Pressed salads – Pressed salads are a cross between raw salads and pickles. Vegetables are mixed with salt or brine and pressed like pickles but stand for less time so they remain crunchy like salads. Pressed salads are made with less salt than pickles. While pickles are served in small amounts, pressed salads can be served in quantities closer to raw salad.

Containers – Pickle in a deep container that will not leak. While vegetables are pickling, they must be surrounded completely by the medium; contact with air can cause spoiling. Three types of pickle containers are described and illustrated.

Japanese pickle press – A press is a special tool (usually plastic) to make pickles through pressure. Many sizes are available; a common size holds about two and one-half quarts. The lid screws on and has an adjustable spring which applies pressure to a disc. The pressure can be adjusted for different types of pickles; for example, strong pressure for pressed pickles and light pressure for brine pickles.

Crock with a weighted plate – This press can be assembled from common kitchen utensils. Ingredients are packed into a large container of ceramic or glass, such as a crock or a large bowl. A plate which fits inside the container without touching the sides is placed on top of the ingredients. A heavy weight, like a gallon jar of water or a heavy rock, may be put on the plate to apply a lot of pressure, as when making pressed pickles. A medium weight, like a small jar of water or a light rock, may be put on the plate to apply just enough pressure to keep the vegetables under the liquid, as when making brine pickles. The weight may be left off so there is only the pressure from the plate, as when making bran pickles. A clean cloth is placed over the entire container to keep out dust.

Two jars – Use two jars when pickling vegetables in brine. The small jar fits inside the large jar and keeps the vegetables submerged. To use, pack vegetables into a gallon jar. Cover with brine. Slip a plastic lid from a storage container inside the jar. Rest lid on top of the vegetables. (This lid will keep all the vegetables down.) Fit the small jar into the large jar so it rests on the plastic lid. Screw on the lid of the large jar. If the lid of the large jar does not hold down the small jar, fill the small jar with water to apply enough weight to keep the vegetables submerged.

Bowl with weighted plate

Japanese pickle press

Two jars

Bran Pickles

Procedure – Bran mixture: Roast bran and salt together in a dry pan (no oil) until fragrant, about 15 minutes. Stir often to prevent burning and to smooth out lumps. Cover and cool completely.

Pickling: Wash vegetables and drain until dry. Cut or leave whole as directed. Use a wide mouth crock or jar, at least a 2 quart size. Press a one-inch layer of the bran mixture in the bottom of the container. Place a layer of vegetables on top so they do not touch each other. Cover completely with bran mixture, press down. Repeat layers, ending with bran mixture. Press down firmly. Place a small flat plate or board on bran. Cover container with a cloth. Remove pickles from the container after the indicated time, and brush off bran. If not serving immediately, store in a covered container in the refrigerator. Don't wash until immediately before slicing. When ready to serve, wash, pat dry, and slice into bite-sized pieces such as half-rounds, logs, thin paper-cut slices, or diagonals.

Bran mixture

1 cup salt per 5 cups rice bran or wheat bran

Vegetables – Use individually or in any combination desired.

red radish, whole – 8 to 12 hours
cucumber, peeled, 2-inch rounds – 8 to 12 hours
cucumber, peeled, whole – 12 to 18 hours
radish greens, whole – 8 to 12 hours
daikon radish, 2-inch rounds – 12 to 18 hours
daikon radish, whole (1½-inch diameter) – 24 to 30 hours
cabbage, leaf – 8 to 12 hours
cabbage, whole and cored – 12 hours for the outer leaves;
    remove pickled outer leaves and replace cabbage head
    in bran to continue pickling
celery, whole or halved – 8 to 12 hours
bok choy, whole or halved – 8 to 12 hours
watermelon rind, ¼ to ½-inch thick pieces of the white
    part of the rind – 4 to 6 hours

Comments – Bran pickles are often referred to as nuka pickles. Nuka means rice bran. If you can't find rice bran, wheat bran or oat bran work well. In Japan, nuka pickle barrels are kept a long time to make pickles over many years with the same nuka. Pickles are made often, and the wet mixture is stirred daily to ensure that it will last. In America, salt bran pickling is a new art. This recipe was adapted by Cornellia Aihara so that it would be easier for Americans to succeed in making pickles. The bran is dry and very salty, so it will keep well.

Vegetables are pickled in large rather than serving-sized pieces because small pieces absorb too much salt, shrink, and lose their shape. Pickle a small amount of vegetables at a time and remove from the pickling container after the initial fermentation. Pickles are done when they begin to shrink and change color and the salt has permeated them. After removing from the bran, the vegetables will continue to pickle somewhat until they are washed. After washing, use them; washed pickles spoil easily.

The new bran mixture is very dry, and the first batches of pickles will turn out salty. So at first, pickle only a few vegetables at a time (like 4 radishes) and use within 2 days. In time, the bran will become soft from the juices drawn out from the vegetables, and the pickles will taste less salty. When the mixture becomes very wet, roast more bran and salt and mix completely with the old bran mixture.

Keep mixture at room temperature in a cool place. Try to tend daily, especially as the mixture becomes more wet, mixing top to bottom. Before placing vegetables in, dump out all the bran. Mix top to bottom. Then layer bran, vegetables, bran. If you must be away, the bran mixture will keep for about one month untended: Remove all vegetables, press down the bran and sprinkle 1 Tbsp. dry salt per 5 to 6 cups of bran on top. The mixture may be refrigerated in hot weather. Remove any mold that develops on the bran. If the bran smells good, it can still be used.

A large container can be used to pickle many vegetables. A five gallon crock with 15 to 20 cups of bran works well for pickling whole vegetables such as daikon or cabbage and when making pickles for many people on a daily basis.

Salt Brine Pickles and Pressed Salads

Procedure – Boil water and salt until the salt has dissolved. Cool completely. Pack vegetables tightly in container. Cover vegetables completely with the brine. Apply enough weight to keep the vegetables submerged. Ferment or press at room temperature for the time indicated. Remove from brine when serving.

Cucumber pickles – Ferment 3 to 4 days. Yield: about 2 quarts.

---

brine of 5 cups water and 10 tsp. salt
20 three-inch pickling cucumbers, whole (or 15 five-inch)
1 clove garlic, thinly sliced; optional
2 sprigs fresh dill, whole; optional

Cucumber and onion pickles – Ferment 3 to 4 days. Yield: about 2 quarts.

---

brine of 5 cups water and 10 tsp. salt
20 three-inch pickling cucumbers, whole (or 15 five-inch)
1 large onion, large crescents

Onion, turnip, and radish pickles – Ferment 3 to 4 days. Yield: about 1 quart.

---

brine of 2 cups water and 4 tsp. salt
1 large onion, large crescents
8 large red radishes, halved or quartered
4 medium turnips, thin quarter rounds

Cabbage, cucumber, and carrot pressed salad – Press 4 to 5 hours or longer. Yield: about 4 cups lightly packed salad.

---

brine of 1 cup water and 1 tsp. salt
½ small cabbage (core remove), shredded
1 medium cucumber, thin quarter rounds
½ small carrot, grated

Lettuce and carrot pressed salad – Press 1 to 2 hours or longer. Yield: about 4 cups lightly packed salad.

---

brine of 1 cup water and 1 tsp. salt
1 small (or ½ medium) lettuce, shredded
2 medium scallions, thin rounds
½ small carrot, grated

Comments – Making brine pickles is perhaps the easiest and most familiar of the pickling techniques covered here. It works beautifully with pickling cucumbers, but root vegetables also pickle well. Almost any vegetable can be pickled with this procedure; just make sure to keep vegetables submerged while pickling. Any of the containers described on page 132 can be used with good results.

The brine used for salt brine pickles contains 2 tsp. salt per 1 cup water. The brine used for pressed salads contains 1 tsp. salt per 1 cup water. Use enough brine to cover the vegetables by ¼ inch, and enough weight to keep the vegetables submerged. As the vegetables pickle they will shrink and release some water, so the amount of liquid will increase.

Pickles will keep about 2 months in the refrigerator and will continue to ferment somewhat after the initial fermentation. Some pickles may turn soft, especially if the vegetables were old to begin with. If white mold develops, scrape it off; you can eat the pickles if they smell good. If mold occurs while pickling, the brine does not have enough salt or the vegetables were not fresh. If mold occurs while pickles are in the refrigerator, the pickles are becoming too old.

Pressed salads are easy to make with salt brine. Use a Japanese pickle press or a bowl with a weight. Press salad longer, up to 24 hours, for a slightly pickled salad.

Try other vegetables for pickles and salads. Carrots, celery, and yellow squash make good pickles; lettuce with celery or red bell pepper make a good pressed salad.

Soy Sauce Brine Pickles and Pressed Salads

Procedure – Bring soy sauce and water to a boil. Cool completely. Pack vegetables tightly in a container. Cover with the brine. Weight to keep the vegetables submerged. Ferment or press at room temperature for the time indicated. Remove from brine when serving.

Onion, radish, and carrot pickles – Ferment 3 to 4 days. Yield: about 1 quart.

---

brine of ½ cup soy sauce and 1 cup water
1 large onion, large crescents
8 medium red radishes, thick rounds
1 medium carrot, thin diagonals

Daikon pickles – Ferment 3 to 4 days. Yield: about 1 quart.

---

brine of ½ cup soy sauce and 1 cup water
2 medium daikon radishes, logs, thin half rounds, or thin
    paper-cut slices

Lettuce, cucumber, and scallion pressed salad – Press 1 to 2 hours or longer. Yield: about 4 cups lightly packed salad.

---

brine of 1 Tbsp. soy sauce and ¼ cup water
1 small (or ½ medium) lettuce, shredded
2 medium scallions, thin rounds
1 medium cucumber, thin quarter rounds

Comments – Root and cut vegetables make good soy sauce pickles. Vegetables will absorb the soy sauce color, but are very tasty. Any of the containers described on page 132 can be used with good results. Vegetables need to be kept under the brine but don't need a lot of pressure.

The brine used for soy sauce pickles contains 2 parts water to 1 part soy sauce. Boiling the brine prevents molding. Use enough brine to cover the vegetables; as they pickle, they will shrink and release water, which will increase the amount of liquid. The brine can be used for second and third batches of pickles. After all the pickles have been eaten, bring the brine to a boil and add more soy sauce. For an original brine of ½ cup soy sauce and 1 cup water, add ¼ cup soy sauce.

Pickles will keep about 2 months in the refrigerator. After the initial fermentation they will be crunchy, but in 10 days, they will soften. They will continue to pickle in the refrigerator, and become more flavorful.

Salads pressed in soy sauce brine are delicious. It is my favorite way to prepare pressed salad. Vegetables will keep their own colors because they are pressed for a short time. Use 1 part soy sauce to 3 to 4 parts water for brine. You can use the brine without boiling; a salad pressed a short time will not mold. Use a pickle press or bowl with a weight to make salad pressed in soy sauce brine.

Try other root vegetables to make pickles, such as turnips or rutabagas. Use singly or in combination with onion. Cabbage, carrots, and radishes make good pressed salads, too.

Pressed Pickles and Salads

Procedure – Mix thinly sliced vegetables with salt thoroughly, scrunching vegetables by hand to soften them. If you have a suribachi, use it to mix the vegetables and salt, kneading them against the sides of the suribachi. If your suribachi is small, mix proportional amounts of vegetables and salt in quantities that will fit.

Pack tightly into a Japanese pickle press. If using bay leaves, place 2 cups of the vegetable and salt mixture in the press and place a small bay leaf on top. Repeat layers ending with a bay leaf on top. Place cover on the press, screw down, and press strongly. Water from the vegetables will rise and cover them. Ferment or press at room temperature for the time indicated. Bubbles will arise in 24 to 30 hours. Remove liquid from portion to be served.

Pressed cabbage pickles – Ferment 3 to 4 days. Yield: about 4 cups tightly packed pickles.

---

1 large cabbage (core removed), shredded thinly
½ to ¾ tsp. salt per 4 cups lightly packed shredded
    cabbage
bay leaves; optional

Pressed Chinese cabbage pickles – Ferment 3 to 4 days. Yield: about 4 cups tightly packed pickles.

---

1 large Chinese cabbage;
    core, finely minced
    leaves, shredded thinly
½ to ¾ tsp. salt per 4 cups lightly packed shredded
    cabbage

Pressed lettuce and cucumber salad – Press 1 to 2 hours or longer. Yield: about 4 cups lightly packed salad.

1 small (or ½ medium) lettuce, shredded
1 medium cucumber, thin quarter rounds
½ tsp. salt

Pressed Chinese cabbage and radish salad – Press 4 to 5 hours or longer. Yield: about 4 cups lightly packed salad.

6 medium Chinese cabbage leaves, shredded
4 large radishes, thin rounds
½ tsp. salt

Comments – Pressing vegetables with salt works best for watery vegetables like cabbage, radishes, and cucumbers. Pressure and salt draw out water from the vegetables. Dense root vegetables like carrots and turnips have less water and should be used in combination with cabbage rather than alone.

It is important to mix the vegetables and salt well. When you knead the vegetables against the sides of a suribachi, the vegetables soften and the salt permeates easily. If you don't have a suribachi, double the amount of salt called for in the recipes.

A Japanese pickle press gives the best results for this procedure because it applies strong pressure which draws out water. If you don't have a Japanese pickle press, you can use a bowl with a weight. Increase the amount of salt to 1 tsp. salt per 4 cups lightly packed shredded vegetables for pickles and to ¾ tsp. salt for salad. Pack into a bowl and place a plate on top of the vegetables. Weight with a heavy rock or bottle of water. Cover with a clean cloth. (More details on page 132.)

Check to make sure the liquid is rising to cover the vegetables. For pickles, if liquid doesn't cover the vegetables after 4 hours, add salted brine to cover (2 tsp. salt per 1 cup water). If liquid doesn't rise to cover the vegetables, it could be from too little salt; too little pressure; vegetables and salt mixed inadequately; or vegetables being too cold at the start. If the liquid did rise and mold developed, too little salt was used. Vegetables must be covered with liquid or they may spoil.

Pressed pickles will keep for up to 2 months. After the initial fermentation of 3 to 4 days, pack tightly into clean jars and refrigerate to slow down the fermentation. At first, the pickles will be slightly crisp, but they will soften after 5 days and become more flavorful.

When making pressed salads by this method, a pickle press will give better results than a bowl with a weight because a press will help draw out water more effectively. Salads can be pressed up to 24 hours for a slightly fermented salad. Longer pressing time will also draw out more water.

Try making other types of pickles and pressed salads. Mix cabbage with cucumbers or scallions for pickles. Cut daikon radish into matchsticks for pickles. Use lettuce or cabbage alone or with radishes, scallions, turnips, or carrots for salads.

Breads

Flour – Whole wheat flour is a basic ingredient in breads, but other flours such as rye flour, cornmeal, and buckwheat flour can be used. Since they have less gluten than whole wheat flour, they are often used with whole wheat flour. Loaf breads should contain at least 50% whole wheat flour in order to rise. For breads that don't rise as much, like biscuits or pancakes, these various flours can be used alone or with less whole wheat flour.

Leavening – Yeast and baking soda are often used to leaven breads. Both are made through refining and sometimes by chemical processes. A better way to leaven breads is through the use of airborne yeasts. The air contains many beneficial bacteria and yeasts. They feed on carbohydrates, and during lengthy contact with the dough, cause the carbohydrate molecules to change from long chains to short chains. The bread rises due to the active growing yeasts, making it more digestible because the carbohydrates are more broken down. In this section, most of the breads do not contain commercial yeast. Yet, they rise because they have a resting period when the dough has contact with airborne yeasts. These naturally leavened breads are more chewy and are very flavorful.

Oil – Oil may be added to give a rich texture and more flavor. It is mixed into dough in one of two ways. Add to flour by rubbing between hands until uniformly mixed; then add liquid. Or, thoroughly mix oil with liquid; then add flour. Different oils or nut butters can be used to give different flavors.

Salt – Salt enhances the flavor and helps maintain the acid-alkaline balance. It toughens the gluten in kneaded breads, giving the bread more texture and elasticity for rising. Salt controls the growth of yeast.

Ingredients – For best results, all ingredients (except the first warm water for the yeast) should be used at room temperature. If any ingredient is very cold, it may slow down the yeast; if any ingredient is very hot, it may kill the yeast. Leftovers such as noodle water, cooked grains, and cooked vegetables like squash can be used well in breads. To make sweet dessert breads, add dried fruits, nuts, or natural sweeteners such as barley malt or rice syrup.

Proportion of flour to water – The higher the proportion of flour to water, the stiffer the dough. Loaf breads, crackers, and chapatis have more flour than batter breads and biscuits, which are moist. Since different flours absorb different amounts of water, keep the end result in mind while mixing. For example, kneaded loaf doughs should be firm and not sticky; biscuit doughs should be thick and wet; pancake batter should be thin and pourable.

Mixing ingredients – There are two ways to mix doughs. Liquid and ingredients other than flour are mixed; then flour is kneaded in. Or, flour and ingredients other than water are mixed; then water is added. Stiffer breads are often mixed by adding flour last; batter breads, by adding water last.

Kneading – Loaf bread dough is kneaded to develop gluten, which gives it rising ability. The dough is kneaded until it is no longer sticky, but feels smooth, like an earlobe. It will take at least 10 to 15 minutes of kneading. You can knead on a lightly floured surface or in a bowl at least twice the size of the dough. When kneading flour into dough, it is easier to place the dough on top of the flour and knead, rather than dumping the flour on top of the dough to knead. Be careful not to add too much flour at a time or the dough will be hard to knead.

Kneading stretches the dough and involves a whole-body move-ment. Basically, push the dough away from you with the heels of the

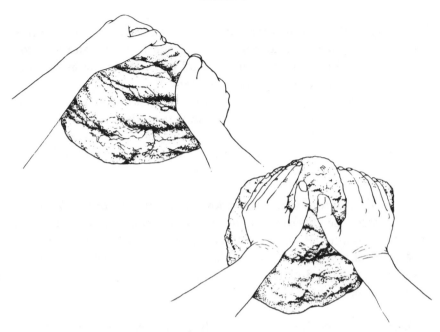

hands, turn it one quarter turn, and pick up the far edge, folding it towards you. Push it away again, turn, fold, etc. To make kneading in a bowl easier, place the bowl on the floor, kneel, and sit on your heels. Raise your body up and back while pulling and folding. Lower your body and lean forward while pushing dough. This movement prevents aching shoulders.

Rising or resting dough – Let dough stand before baking. Quick breads should rest 15 to 30 minutes to allow the ingredients to mix and swell. Kneaded loaf breads will rise over a period of hours. Unyeasted doughs will come in contact with airborne yeasts so they will rise. Yeasted doughs will rise due to the activity of the leaven. Check dough periodically while rising; let it rise until it has expanded but still has a pleasant fermenting smell without smelling sour. The rising time will vary. In the summer, yeasted doughs will rise in 2 to 4 hours and unyeasted ones in 8 to 10 hours. In the winter, allow 6 to 8 hours for yeasted doughs and up to 24 hours for unyeasted. Batter breads can be set in the sun to rise and will rise in 3 to 4 hours. During the time of rising or resting, cover the bowl with a damp cloth to prevent the dough from drying out or crusting.

Forming the loaves – After the dough has risen, cut dough with a table knife and form it into loaf shapes. Smooth creases and lines for an even crust. Fit dough into oiled bread pans, about three-quarters full, and gently press into corners as needed.

Place filled bread pans in a warm oven for 1 hour to rise and warm before baking. An oven with a pilot light provides a good temperature. If your oven has no pilot or is electric, heat the oven for a few minutes, turn it off, and place bread inside. Remove bread while preheating oven to baking temperature.

Baking – Slash tops with a sharp knife, making one or two ½-inch-deep, lengthwise cuts to allow the bread to expand while baking and to avoid cracking. Bake in a preheated oven. Loaf breads are done when they are browned, cooked throughout, and produce a hollow sound when tapped on the bottom. Muffins or crackers are done when the bottoms are browned.

Cooling – The cooling-off is actually a time for the bread to finish baking. Loaf breads take at least an hour to cool, while biscuits or muffins take 10 minutes. Bread tastes good while hot, but can be gummy and hard to digest. Let cool completely before slicing and eating: Remove from baking pans and place on a rack.

Problems – To make good bread, you need to use a recipe over and over to learn how all of your unique factors work together, such as the kind of flour, the size of the pans, and the oven temperature. If the dough doesn't rise, either it is too cold, or the yeast is inactive. Set in a warmer place and let rise longer; up to 24 hours for un-yeasted bread and up to 12 for yeasted. If, after baking, the crust is too hard, the oven heat was too hot, or the bread baked too long. Try steaming the bread or cutting into croutons. If the crust is hard but the inside is gummy or doughy, the heat was too high and the cooking time too short. Slice thinly and toast. If bread sticks to the pans, the pans were oiled too lightly. Use these chunks of bread for dipping into soup.

Oiling pans – Oil pans lightly before filling. Place pans in the oven for 5 minutes to heat. Oil will spread easily with a brush.

Loaf Breads, Naturally Leavened

Procedure – Place all ingredients except flour into a bowl. Mix well until smooth and without lumps, using a wire whisk if necessary. Add whole wheat flour by the cupful until you can no longer stir it. Add more whole wheat flour, mixing by hand, until the dough is no longer sticky. Knead until smooth, 10 to 15 minutes adding small amounts of flour as necessary. Cover bowl with a damp cloth. Place in a warm spot. Let rise until the dough has expanded, but still smells sweet; 8 to 10 hours in hot weather; up to 24 hours in cold weather. Form into loaves. Place into oiled loaf pans. Let rise 1 hour in a warm oven. Remove from oven. Slit tops. Preheat oven to 350 degrees. Bake for 1 to 1½ hours, depending on size of loaves.

Wheat bread – 3 small loaves

4 cups water
2 Tbsp. corn oil
1½ tsp. salt
11 to 14 cups whole wheat flour

Grain bread – 3 small loaves

2 cups cooled, cooked grain
4 cups water
1¼ tsp. salt (assuming grain cooked with salt)
12 to 15 cups whole wheat flour

Comments – This basic bread can be varied easily. Try replacing 4 cups whole wheat flour with 4 cups rye flour, or with 1 cup buckwheat flour and 3 cups cornmeal. Try various grains with various flours, such as cooked barley with wheat and rye flours, or cooked rice with cornmeal and wheat flours. Use at least 50% whole wheat flour and add the flour of smallest quantity first. For other variations use leftover noodle water; different oils or sesame butter; or add raisins or roasted nuts.

Loaf Breads, Yeasted

Procedure – Soften yeast in ½ cup warm (80°F) water. Add a small amount of flour. Let stand 10 to 15 minutes until bubbly. Add the rest of the warm water, oil, and salt. Mix well. Add whole wheat flour by the cupful until you can no longer stir it. Add more whole wheat flour, mixing by hand, until the dough is no longer sticky. Knead until smooth, 10 to 15 minutes, adding small amounts of flour as necessary. Cover bowl with a damp cloth. Place in a warm spot. Let rise until the dough has expanded, but still smells sweet: 2 to 4 hours in hot weather; 6 to 8 hours in cold weather. Form into loaves. Place into oiled loaf pans. Let rise 1 hour in a warm oven. Remove from oven. Slit tops. Preheat oven to 350 degrees. Bake for 1 to 1¼ hours, depending on the size of the loaves.

Yeasted bread – 4 small loaves

1 tsp. dry yeast
½ cup warm water (80°F)
2 Tbsp. whole wheat flour (for yeast mixture)
5 cups warm water
¼ cup corn oil
1¾ to 2 tsp. salt
14 to 17 cups whole wheat flour

Comments – Yeasted bread is faster to make than unyeasted bread. It is a lighter bread which is nice for guests or holidays. Vary the recipe by combining different flours with the whole wheat flour such as 5 cups rye flour; 4 cups rolled oats; or 2 cups rye flour and 2 cups cornmeal. Make sure loaf contains at least 50% whole wheat flour so the dough will rise. Also try other oils, or adding leftover noodle water. Roasted nuts or dried fruits can be added. Cooked pureed vegetables such as squash or carrots can be added to liquid for a vegetable bread.

Batter Breads

Procedure – Rub oil into flour(s) by hand until uniformly mixed. Add salt. Mix in grain, if used, separating the kernels. Add water until the dough is moist yet thick. Beat well. Cover the bowl with a damp cloth. Place in a warm spot. Let rise until the dough is bubbly but still smells sweet: 3 to 4 hours in direct sunlight; 6 to 8 hours indoors in hot weather; up to 12 hours in cold weather. Pour into a well-oiled baking pan. Bake 1¼ hours at 350 degrees.

Cornmeal batter bread – 9″ x 13″ pan

5 cups cornmeal
5 cups whole wheat flour
¼ cup corn oil
1 tsp. salt
2 cups cooled cooked rice; optional
7 to 8 cups water

Wheat batter bread – 9″ x 13″ pan

8 cups whole wheat flour
¼ cup corn oil
1 tsp. salt
4 to 5 cups water

Comments – Batter bread is easier to make than kneaded bread. The dough is moist and produces a soft bread. Cornbread is very good made by this method, especially when it rises in the sun. A 9″ x 13″ baking pan works well, but loaf pans or muffin tins can be used, too. Oil pans well so bread doesn't stick.

This recipe turns out well with almost any variation. Even the proportions can be changed to more water or flour. I often use up all my leftover flour, grain, and cooking water with this recipe. Other variations include egg: beat 1 egg and mix into the dough just before filling the pan; baking soda: add ¼ tsp soda just before filling pan; or add nuts, raisins, or soymilk.

Flatbreads, Unyeasted

Procedure – Rub oil into flour by hand, smoothing out lumps until uniformly mixed. Add salt and roasted seeds, if used. Add water until the dough holds together without being sticky. Knead on lightly floured surface until smooth, about 5 minutes. Let dough rest 15 minutes or longer.

For chapatis, make 1½-inch-diameter balls. Roll out on lightly floured surface, dusting dough with flour so rolling pin doesn't stick. Roll each ball into a 5-inch round chapati, about ¼-inch thick. Place in a dry skillet (no oil). Toast over medium heat until there are a few brown spots, 2 to 3 minutes each side; they will cook faster as the skillet becomes hotter.

For crackers, roll out on floured surface, lightly dusting dough with flour so the rolling pin doesn't stick. Roll out to ⅜-inch thickness or less. Place on an oiled baking sheet. Score into cracker shapes. Prick each cracker with a fork. Bake 25 to 30 minutes at 350 degrees.

Unyeasted crackers or chapatis – 16 five-inch chapatis, or 2 baking sheets (9″ x 13″) of crackers

---

3 Tbsp. corn oil
5 cups whole wheat flour
½ tsp. salt
½ cup roasted sesame seeds, page 127; optional
1 to 1½ cups cool water

Comments – Unyeasted crackers or chapatis are fast to make. The dough can rest longer, up to 12 hours; longer resting times make the dough rise. The thinner the dough is rolled out, the faster it will cook. Chapatis are better when thicker because they are softer and more pliable. Crackers are better when thinner because they are more crisp. For variety, try other flours and seeds, such as whole wheat and rye flours with caraway seeds, or whole wheat flour with sunflower seeds.

Flatbreads, Boiling Water

Procedure – Mix boiling water, oil, and salt. Whip with a fork or wire whisk. Add flour. Mix well. Add roasted seeds, if used. Knead on lightly floured surface 2 to 3 minutes until smooth, kneading in more flour if needed. Refrigerate for 30 minutes with a damp cloth over the bowl.

For rolling out chapatis and crackers, follow the same procedures as for Flatbreads, Unyeasted, page 150.

> **Crackers or chapatis** – 10 five-inch chapatis, or 1 sheet (9″ x 13″) of crackers
>
> 1 cup boiling water
> 2 Tbsp. corn oil
> ¼ tsp. salt
> 3 cups whole wheat flour
> ¼ cup roasted sesame seeds, page 127; optional

Comments – Crackers or chapatis made with boiling water dough are light and tender, almost like cookies. The dough is sticky and has less flour than unyeasted flatbread dough, but by refrigerating, the dough becomes easier to work with. If the dough tears when rolling, pick up and knead together, then roll out again. It usually won't tear a second time. Try other flours and seeds, such as rye and wheat flours with caraway seeds, or barley and wheat flours with sunflower seeds.

Crackers and chapatis also can be made from the yeasted loaf bread recipe. Just make dough, let rise, roll out, and cook as outlined.

Muffins

Procedure – Rub oil into flour by hand, smoothing out lumps until uniformly mixed. Add salt. Add water and mix thoroughly with a wooden spoon. Batter should be runny. Let the batter rest 20 to 30 minutes. Batter will thicken somewhat but still will be thin. Fill heated, well-oiled muffin tins. Bake 45 to 55 minutes at 400 degrees.

Whole wheat muffins – 12 muffins

2½ cups whole wheat pastry flour
2 Tbsp. arrowroot powder or brown rice flour
1 Tbsp. corn oil
¼ tsp. salt
2 cups water

Buckwheat muffins – 12 muffins

1½ cups buckwheat flour
1 cup whole wheat pastry flour
1 Tbsp. corn oil
¼ tsp. salt
2 cups water

Comments – Muffins are moist. The batter is thin and also can be used to make pancakes. For variety use different flours such as cornmeal, rye flour, or barley flour, alone or in combination. Water left over from cooking noodles makes good muffins. Egg, baking soda, or nuts may be added to the batter right before filling tins.

Muffins can be filled with cooked vegetables or fruit. To fill, spoon tins one-third full of batter; add 1 Tbsp. filling; spoon batter to top of tin. Try cooked mashed winter squash or sweet potatoes in the whole wheat muffins, or applesauce in the buckwheat muffins.

Biscuits

Procedure – Rub oil into flour by hand, smoothing out lumps until uniformly mixed. Add salt and rolled oats, if used. Add water and mix thoroughly with a wooden spoon. Batter should be wet. Let batter rest and thicken 20 to 30 minutes. Batter will hold its shape when spooned onto a well-oiled baking sheet. Bake 35 to 40 minutes at 350 degrees.

Cornmeal biscuits – 14 biscuits

1½ cups cornmeal
1 cup whole wheat pastry flour
2 Tbsp. corn oil
¼ tsp. salt
1½ cups water

Whole wheat biscuits – 14 biscuits

2½ cups whole wheat flour or whole wheat pastry flour
2 Tbsp. corn oil
¼ tsp. salt
1½ cups water

Buckwheat and oatmeal biscuits – 14 biscuits

1 cup buckwheat flour
1 cup whole wheat flour
2 Tbsp. corn oil
½ cup rolled oats
¼ tsp. salt
1½ cups water

Comments – Make different kinds of biscuits by using other flours such as rye or barley, or by adding roasted nuts. The whole wheat biscuits can be made into cookies by using pastry flour and adding carob chips or cinnamon and raisins.

Crisps

Procedure – Mix cold water and salt. Add flaked grain. Let stand until water is absorbed, 20 to 25 minutes. Spread thinly on an oiled baking sheet in 3-inch patties. Bake at 350 degrees for 30 to 40 minutes, or until crispy.

Oat crisp – 1 sheet (9″ x 13″) of patties

> 2 cups water
> ¼ tsp. salt
> 3 cups rolled oats

Comments – Oat crisps are a light alternative to flour wafers. When mixing batter, it may seem too wet, yet the flakes will absorb most of the water. If there is liquid remaining, spoon some of the liquid onto each of the patties. For variety use rye or wheat flakes alone or in combination with rolled oats. Oat crisp can be made into a sweet cookie by adding nuts or currants or by replacing water with apple juice.

Pancakes and Waffles

Procedure – Mix water, salt, and grain, if used, separating lumps. Add flour. Lightly mix. Let stand 5 to 10 minutes. Batter should be pourable. For pancakes, ladle onto medium-hot, oiled skillet. Pan-fry the first side for 5 minutes or until bubbles have risen, and the second side 2 to 3 minutes until browned. For waffles, ladle onto heated, well-oiled waffle iron. Bake until browned, 7 to 10 minutes.

Simple pancakes or waffles – 12 four-inch pancakes

2 cups water
2½ to 2¾ cups flour
⅛ tsp. salt
Oil

Pancakes or waffles with grain – 8 four-inch pancakes

1 cup cooled, cooked grain
2 cups water
⅛ tsp. salt
1½ to 2 cups flour
Oil

Comments – Pancakes made with grain are thicker than pancakes made with flour only, which are thin like crepes. Try using various grains and flours: cooked rice with whole wheat flour; cooked rice with buckwheat flour; cooked millet or cooked oatmeal with whole wheat flour. Also try roasting the flour, or adding currants, roasted seeds or nuts. Top pancakes with maple syrup, thinned rice syrup, apple sauce, mashed cooked winter squash, or a nut butter sauce.

Dumplings

Procedure – Mix flour and salt. Add boiling water. Mix well. Knead in bowl for 1 minute. Form into ½-inch diameter balls. Drop into boiling water or soup. Cover pot and simmer 5 minutes. Dumplings are done when they float.

Dumplings – 30 to 35 half-inch diameter dumplings

> 1 cup flour
> pinch salt
> ⅓ cup boiling water

Comments – Dumplings top soups nicely. They are quick to make. Try various flours, such as whole wheat flour, whole wheat pastry flour, rice flour, or buckwheat flour. Also try roasting the flour before mixing the batter.

Desserts and Snacks

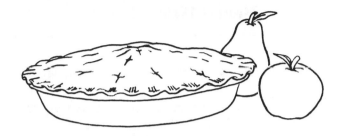

Simple desserts – This book includes desserts which can be made quickly, easily, and in small amounts. Many are cooked on top of the stove and use only one utensil. Some desserts are made with vegetables and use no fruits or sweeteners. There are no cakes or fancy creations with glazes or creams. Recipes for these are available in many gourmet macrobiotic cookbooks (see Suggested Readings, pages 258–259).

Fruits – Wash fresh fruits before cutting. If fruit is not organic, you may wish to peel it. Juices can be used to sweeten desserts, but since juices are pressed from fruit, they are not considered whole foods. Use for special-occasion desserts.

Vegetables – Sweet potatoes, winter squash, and parsnips can be used for desserts. Use leftovers or cook fresh, simmering with salt on top (see page 42). To make vegetables more sweet, simmer 1½ to 2 hours. Use to fill muffins or pies or as an ingredient in puddings, breads, or cookies. Sweet potatoes can be served as a dessert as is, or by topping with roasted almonds or cashews.

Salt – Use a little salt in desserts to balance the high amount of potassium in fruit. Salt also brings out the sweetness.

Baked Whole Fruit

Procedure – Mix stuffing ingredients well, if used. Mixture should be moist and hold its shape. Stuff whole cored fruit or fruit cut in halves and cored. Place water and fruit (stuffed side up) in oiled baking dish. Cover dish. Bake at 400 degrees for 1 hour or until soft.

Baked apples

6 large apples, whole or halved, with cores removed
stuffing: optional;
    2 Tbsp. sesame butter
    2 to 3 tsp. water
    ½ tsp. cinnamon
    ¼ tsp. soy sauce
½ cup boiling water for baking dish

Baked pears

6 large pears, halved and cored
stuffing: optional;
    2 Tbsp. sesame butter or almond butter
    2 to 3 tsp. lemon juice
    ¼ tsp. soy sauce
½ cup boiling water for baking dish

Comments – Baking works well with firm fruits because they hold their shape. Other fruits such as peaches and plums can be baked whole, but become soft and lose their shape.

Baked Fruit with Topping

Procedure – Fill oiled baking dish with fruit. Add water to the dish. Sprinkle grated citrus rind or cinnamon on top of fruit. Make topping by rubbing oil into flour, mixing in rolled oats and salt, and adding water until moistened but still crumbly. Sprinkle topping on fruit. Cover dish. Bake at 400 degrees for 40 to 45 minutes or until fruit is soft.

Baked apples with topping – 9″ x 9″ baking dish

4 cups apples, thinly sliced
¼ cup water for baking dish
½ tsp. grated lemon or orange rind
topping:
    2 Tbsp. corn oil
    ½ cup whole wheat pastry flour
    1 cup rolled oats
    ¼ tsp. salt
    3 to 4 Tbsp. water

Comments – Try baking other fruit, such as pears, peaches, or apples and pears together. Cooked squash can be used, or cooked squash and raw apples together. The topping can be varied by adding ¼ cup grated unsweetened coconut, chopped walnuts, or by sweetening with ¼ cup rice syrup (heat syrup with water, then add to flour and oats topping). If you wish to make the topping more crisp, remove the cover from the pan for the last 15 minutes of baking.

Sauteed Fruit

Procedure – Heat oil in skillet. Add 1 layer of fruit. Saute until browned, 1 to 2 minutes each side. Add water and salt. Cover pan. Bring to a boil. Steam over low heat for 10 minutes or until water is gone.

Sauteed apples – Yield: 2 to 3 cups.

    1 tsp. corn oil
    2 large apples, thinly sliced
    ¼ cup water
    pinch salt

Sauteed pears – Yield: 2 to 3 cups.

    1 tsp. corn oil
    2 large pears, thinly sliced
    ¼ cup water
    pinch salt

Comments – Sauteing fruit works best with firm fruit such as apples and pears. It is good in the fall, and when you want a quick dessert or snack. Vary the recipes by adding a pinch of cinnamon, ginger, or nutmeg when adding the water and salt.

Stewed Dried Fruit Sauces

Procedure – Soak dried fruit 15 to 20 minutes in water. Add salt after soaking. Cover. Bring to a boil. Simmer over low heat for 20 to 30 minutes or until soft. Mash.

Apricot sauce – Yield: 2 cups.

1 cup dried apricots
1½ cups water
½ tsp. salt

Prune sauce – Remove prune pits after cooking. Yield: 2 cups.

1½ cup prunes
1½ cups water
½ tsp. salt

Raisin sauce – Yield: 2 cups.

1½ cups raisins or currants
1½ cups water
½ tsp. salt

Comments – Dried fruit makes a rich sauce. Any dried fruit can be used, singly or in combination. Try to use unsulphured and/or organic dried fruit when possible. Fruit can be blended after cooking for a smoother texture. Serve separately, use as a topping for pancakes or biscuits, to fill muffins, or add to cookies or puddings.

Fruit Sauces

Procedure – Place water in pan. Add fruit. Sprinkle salt on top. Cover. Bring to a boil. Simmer over low heat for the time indicated. Puree in a blender for a smoother texture, or puree in a food mill to remove the skins.

Applesauce – Simmer 30 minutes. Yield: 10 to 12 cups.

1 cup water
3 lbs. apples, cored and chopped
1 tsp. salt

Peach sauce – Simmer 20 minutes. Yield: 10 to 12 cups.

½ cup water
3 lbs. peaches, pitted and chopped
1 tsp. salt

Pear sauce – Simmer 30 minutes. Yield: 10 to 12 cups.

1 cup water
3 lbs. pears, cored and chopped
1 tsp. salt

Comments – These fruit sauces are cooked completely to make a soft sauce. Try other fruits such as plums or mixtures of apples and apricots, or apples, strawberries, and raisins. Make fruit butters by pureeing in a food mill, then simmering in an uncovered pan for 1 to 1½ hours until thick and deep-colored.

Fruit in Clear Sauce

Procedure – Bring water, salt, and raisins to a boil. Simmer 5 to 10 minutes over low heat, until raisins are plump. Add fruit. Bring to a boil. Add dissolved arrowroot. Stir until thick and clear, 1 to 2 minutes. Remove from heat. Add flavoring.

Peaches in sauce – Yield: 4 to 5 cups.

1 cup water
¼ tsp. salt
¼ cup raisins or currants
4 large peaches, pitted and cut into crescents
1 Tbsp. arrowroot dissolved in 2 Tbsp. water
flavoring: ½ tsp. vanilla or lemon extract

Plums in sauce – Yield: 4 to 5 cups.

1 cup water
¼ tsp. salt
¼ cup raisins or currants
6 to 8 medium plums, pitted and sliced
1 Tbsp. arrowroot dissolved in 2 Tbsp. water
flavoring: ½ tsp. vanilla or lemon extract

Comments – These fruit sauces are good using stone fruits, such as peaches, plums, and apricots. Fruit is cooked through yet holds its shape. Try mixing fruits, such as apricots and plums. The raisins and salt make the sauce sweet. If desired, omit raisins and use rice syrup. Bring water, salt, and ¼ cup syrup to a boil, add fruit; continue as outlined. Plums in sauce complements cornmeal biscuits well, page 153.

Fruit with Sauce

Procedure – Bring water, salt, and raisins to a boil. Simmer 5 to 10 minutes over low heat, until raisins are plump. Add dissolved arrowroot, and stir until thick and clear, 1 to 2 minutes. Cool 5 minutes. Pour over fruit.

Strawberries with sauce – Yield: 3 to 4 cups.

1 cup water
¼ tsp. salt
¼ cup raisins or currants
1 Tbsp. arrowroot dissolved in 2 Tbsp. cold water
1 pint strawberries, halved

Cantaloupe with sauce – Yield: 3 to 4 cups.

1 cup water
¼ tsp. salt
¼ cup raisins or currants
1 Tbsp. arrowroot dissolved in 2 Tbsp. cold water
1 medium cantaloupe, peeled, seeded, and cut into
    squares

Comments – These fruit sauces are good with fruits that lose their shape if cooked, such as berries and melons. Try other fruits, such as raspberries or cherries. Or mix fruits: blueberries, cantaloupe, and strawberries. The raisins and salt make a sweet sauce. If desired, omit raisins and use rice syrup. Bring water, salt, and ¼ cup rice syrup to a boil, add dissolved arrowroot, and continue as outlined. These sauces are refreshing in the summer.

Fruit and Grain Puddings

Procedure – Bring liquid to a boil. Add all ingredients except flavoring and nuts, if used. Cover. Bring to a boil. Simmer over low heat for the time indicated. Remove from heat. Stir in flavoring and/or nuts, if used. Puree in blender for a smooth texture, if desired. Cool to set.

Apricot pudding – Simmer 40 minutes. Yield: 4 to 5 cups.

4 cups water
¼ tsp. salt
1 cup rolled oats
½ cup raisins
¼ cup dried apricots
flavoring: ½ tsp. vanilla extract

Rice pudding – Simmer 20 minutes. Yield: 5 to 6 cups.

4 cups apple juice
¼ tsp. salt
2 cups cooked brown rice
¼ tsp. cinnamon
½ cup walnuts, roasted and chopped

Lemon pudding – Simmer 30 minutes. Yield: 5 to 6 cups.

4 cups water
¼ tsp. salt
1 cup millet, washed and drained
4 apples, cored and chopped
½ tsp. grated lemon rind
flavoring: 2 Tbsp. lemon juice

Comments – Puddings made with grain are substantial. Try using other dried fruits, such as peaches with rolled oats; other juices, such as strawberry apple with millet; or other spices, such as ginger or cloves with cooked rice.

Flour Puddings

Procedure – Heat oil in a pan. Add flour(s) to oil and roast until fragrant, 1 to 2 minutes, stirring constantly with the back of a wooden spoon to prevent lumps. Remove from heat and cool 5 to 10 minutes. Add 1 cup of cold liquid. Mix until smooth. Place over medium heat and add the rest of the cold liquid, stirring constantly. Use a wire whisk if necessary to smooth lumps. Add salt. Add spices if used. Cover. Bring to a boil. Simmer over low heat for 30 minutes, stirring once or twice. Remove from heat. Add and mix in sweetener and flavoring if used. Cool to set.

Cornmeal pudding – Yield: 4 to 5 cups.

1 Tbsp. corn oil
1 cup fine cornmeal
4 cups cold apple juice
¼ tsp. salt
½ tsp. cinnamon

Carob pudding – Roast carob powder and flour together. Yield: 4 to 6 cups.

1 Tbsp. corn oil
1 Tbsp. carob powder
1 cup whole wheat pastry flour
4 to 5 cups water
¼ tsp. salt
¼ cup maple syrup
flavoring: ¼ tsp. vanilla extract

Comments – Making a pudding with flour is like making a sweet bechamel sauce. Try brown or sweet brown rice flour; cook in apricot or apple strawberry juice; cook with raisins or currants; use rice or barley malt syrup; or add ginger or lemon extract. Sweet rice flour with rice syrup and lemon extract is good.

Couscous Puddings

Procedure – Bring liquid to a boil. Add other ingredients. Cover. Bring to a rolling boil until grain almost foams out of the pan. Remove from flame. Let stand 10 minutes before serving or removing to a serving dish. Garnish when serving if desired.

Couscous and blueberry pudding – Yield: 5 to 6 cups.

5 cups water
¼ tsp. salt
2 cups couscous
1 pint blueberries

Couscous and squash pudding – Yield: 5 to 6 cups.

5 cups water
⅛ tsp. salt
2 cups couscous
1 cup cooked mashed winter squash
garnish: roasted almonds, page 127

Comments – Couscous is a processed wheat product, made from steamed, refined wheat. Couscous puddings cook quickly; use with ingredients which also cook quickly, such as berries or leftover cooked vegetables. Try replacing water with apple juice, or adding a sweetener such as rice syrup or malt syrup. Sweet potatoes, or strawberries with rice syrup make good couscous puddings.

Kanten Gelled Desserts

Procedure – Bring agar-agar (kanten), liquid, and salt to a boil. Simmer over low heat with lid ajar until agar-agar is dissolved (see comments). If using fruit (other than berries), lemon rind, or sweetener, add next; bring to a boil. If using arrowroot, dilute and add next; stir in and cook until clear, 1 to 2 minutes. Remove from heat. Cool in pan 5 to 10 minutes. Add flavoring and berries, if used. Ladle into serving dishes. Cool at room temperature until jelled, 1 to 1½ hours. If desired, refrigerate for faster jelling.

Peach and apple kanten – Yield: 6 to 7 cups.

1 Tbsp. agar-agar powder
4 cups apple juice, reserve 2 Tbsp. to dissolve arrowroot
¼ tsp. salt
4 medium peaches, pitted and sliced into crescents
1 Tbsp. arrowroot dissolved in 2 Tbsp. apple juice
flavoring: ½ tsp. vanilla extract

Creamy lemon kanten – Yield: 4 cups.

1 Tbsp. agar-agar powder
3 cups water
¼ tsp. salt
½ cup rice syrup
1 tsp. grated lemon peel
1 Tbsp. arrowroot dissolved in 2 Tbsp. water
flavoring: ½ cup lemon juice (1 large lemon)

Orange kanten – Yield: 4 cups.

1 Tbsp. agar-agar powder
2 cups water
¼ tsp. salt
¼ cup rice syrup
flavoring: 2 cups orange juice

Strawberry kanten – Yield: 4 to 5 cups.

---

1 Tbsp. agar-agar powder
3¾ cups water
¼ tsp. salt
¼ cup rice syrup
flavoring: ½ medium lime, juiced
1 pint strawberries, sliced

Comments – Agar-agar (kanten) is a colorless and flavorless sea vegetable which comes in three forms: bars, flakes, and powder. Each form is cooked for a different length of time until it dissolves and each gels a different quantity of liquid. The following proportions are general; check the package of the brand you are using.

Bars – Soak in liquid for 10 minutes; then cook 20 to 30 minutes to dissolve. One package of 2 bars will gel 5 cups liquid.

Flakes – Cook 5 to 10 minutes to dissolve. One tablespoon will gel 1 cup liquid.

Powder – Cook 2 to 3 minutes to dissolve. One tablespoon will gel 4 cups liquid.

Use different juices and fruits such as apricot juice and cherries, or grape juice and blueberries. Use other sweeteners such as malt syrup or maple syrup or omit sweetening for a more subtle dessert. Use arrowroot to make a creamy kanten or omit it for a clear kanten. Use more kanten or less liquid for a more solid or quicker-gelling kanten. Cook fruits such as plums, apricots, and peaches into kanten; pour cooked kanten over fruits such as berries, cherries, and grapes. Also, kanten can be gelled in a baked pie crust for a clear pie, page 177. Let kanten cool slightly before pouring into a baked and cooled crust to gel.

Drop Cookies

Procedure – Mix oil or nut butter and sweetener together. Add liquid, and mix well. Add salt. Add spices, extracts, dried fruit, and nuts, and mix. Add rolled oats and/or flours, mixing well. Place damp cloth over bowl. Let dough rest 10 to 15 minutes. Spoon onto a well-oiled baking sheet and flatten into 2-inch cookies, about ½-inch thick. Bake at 350 degrees for 20 to 30 minutes or until bottoms are browned. Cool on a rack.

Applesauce and oatmeal cookies – Soft dough. Makes 20 two-inch cookies.

> 2 Tbsp. corn oil
> 1 cup applesauce (sweetener)
> 1 cup water
> ¼ tsp. salt
> ½ tsp. cinnamon
> 2 cups rolled oats
> 1 cup whole wheat pastry flour

Squash and almond cookies – Soft dough. Drop cookies onto sheet, and place one almond on top of each before baking. Makes 20 two-inch cookies.

> 2 Tbsp. corn oil
> 2 cups cooked winter squash, mashed (sweetener)
> 1 cup water
> ¼ tsp. salt
> ½ tsp. cinnamon
> 2½ cups whole wheat pastry flour
> almonds

Oatmeal and walnut cookies – Uses the natural sweetness of the apple juice and dried fruit. Firm dough. Makes 40 two-inch cookies.

¼ cup corn oil
2 cups water or apple juice
½ tsp. salt
½ tsp. cinnamon
½ cup raisins or currants
½ cup walnuts, chopped
2 cups rolled oats
3 cups whole wheat pastry flour

Sweet nut butter cookies – Firm dough. Try peanut butter and barley malt syrup, sesame butter and rice syrup, or almond butter and maple syrup. If sweeteners or butters are hard, heat with one-half of the liquid until softened; then mix with other ingredients. Makes 40 two-inch cookies.

½ cup nut or seed butter
¼ cup sweetener
1 cup water
½ tsp. salt
¼ tsp. vanilla extract
3 cups whole wheat pastry flour

Comments – Dough for drop cookies can be either soft or firm. Soft doughs have more liquid, but should hold their shape when placed on the baking sheet. Firm doughs have more flour but should be pliable and not too stiff when placed on the baking sheet. Doughs can be varied by using different ingredients. Different fruit butters can be used; as can other nuts, sweeteners, nut butters, spices, or dried fruit. Drop cookies can be made from the batters for biscuits, page 153, or crisps, page 154.

Rolled Cookies

Procedure – Mix oil, sweetener, water, and extract, if used. Heat if necessary until the mixture is soft, then let it cool. Sift dry ingredients into a separate bowl. Make a well in the center of the dry ingredients. Add the liquid ingredients to the center. Mix until just moistened. Don't overmix. Place a damp cloth over the bowl. Refrigerate for 1 hour. Roll out on a lightly floured surface to ¼-inch thickness, lightly dusting the top of the dough to prevent the rolling pin from sticking. Dip cookie cutter in flour and cut cookies. Place cookies on oiled baking sheet. Bake at 375 degrees for 10 to 15 minutes or until slightly browned.

Simple rolled cookies – 8 dozen two-inch cookies.

½ cup corn oil
½ cup rice syrup
¾ cup water
1 tsp. vanilla extract
4 cups whole wheat pastry flour
1 tsp. cinnamon
1 tsp. salt

Comments – This recipe makes a light, tender cookie which can be varied easily. Try maple syrup, lemon or almond extract, or dry ginger. Replace 2 cups of pastry flour with 2 cups brown rice flour or sweet brown rice flour for a more crisp cookie. Decorate with seeds or currants before baking.

Dough should be moist; refrigerating will help make it workable. Don't add too much flour while rolling out, or cookies can become tough. When cutting the cookies, try to use as much of the dough as possible. Any small bits of leftover uncut dough can be gently pressed together and rolled out again for cutting.

Pressed Pie Crust

Procedure – Mix flour and salt. Rub in oil by hand, smoothing lumps. Add rolled oats, and mix. Add water gradually, by sprinkling over the dough with the fingers. Mix water into flour, oats, and oil mixture with a fork. Sprinkle more water and mix gently, just until dough holds together. Don't overmix or knead as the crust can become tough. Press into an oiled pie tin with the fingers. Bake at 350 degrees for 15 to 20 minutes or until firm. Then fill and bake as per filling recipe, page 176.

Pressed pie crust – 1 crust for 9-inch pie.

2 cups whole wheat flour
¼ tsp. salt
¼ cup corn oil
½ cup rolled oats
6 to 7 Tbsp. cold water

Comments – Pressed pie crust is flaky because of the rolled oats. It is thicker than rolled pie crust and is very good with vegetable or gelled fillings. When filling with gelled fillings, bake 30 to 35 minutes or until browned. Cool, then fill.

Vary this recipe by using part sweet brown rice flour or brown rice flour. Use ¼ cup rice flour to 1¾ cups whole wheat flour. Shredded, unsweetened coconut or chopped nuts may be added.

Rolled Pie Crust

Procedure – Mix flour and salt. Rub in oil by hand, smoothing lumps. Add a small amount of water by sprinkling over dough with the fingers. Mix water into flour and oil mixture with a fork. Sprinkle more water and gently mix until dough holds together. Add only enough water so dough sticks together and is still springy. If dough feels sticky, there is too much water. Don't overmix or knead, or crust may become tough.

Separate into 2 parts. Roll the first part on a lightly floured surface, dusting dough with flour so rolling pin doesn't stick. Roll to 12-inch diameter, ¼-inch thick. Place in an oiled pie tin. Trim any extra dough which extends over the edge of the pie tin with a table knife. Bake bottom crust at 350 degrees for 10 to 30 minutes (see comments).

Fill with pie filling. For pie with top crust, roll out second part. Place on top of filling, and again, trim any extending dough. Moisten between the top and bottom crust. Seal edges together by pinching between the thumb and forefinger. Slit top crust to allow steam to escape. Bake as per any filling recipe, page 176. For a one-crust pie, either halve the recipe or bake the second half as cookies (see comments).

Rolled pie crust – 2 crusts for 9-inch pie.

3 cups whole wheat pastry flour
¼ tsp. salt
2 to 3 Tbsp. corn oil
⅔ cups cold water

Comments – This basic crust makes a light whole wheat pie crust. Use more oil to make crust more flaky. Try brown rice flour or sweet brown rice flour with whole wheat pastry flour to make a crisper crust. Use ½ cup rice flour and 2½ cups pastry flour.

If the dough tears while rolling or placing into pie pan, patch it rather than kneading together and rolling out again as overworking the dough can make it tough. Trimmings can be sprinkled with cinnamon and baked as cookies.

You may bake the bottom crust before filling if you wish, but it is not necessary. However, if the filling is wet, such as berries, lightly pre-bake bottom crust so it won't become soggy. Prick holes in crust so air can escape and bake at 350 degrees for 10 minutes. If dough will be used for a gelled filling, prick holes in it and bake at 350 degrees for 20 to 30 minutes or until browned. Cool, then fill.

Pie Fillings

Procedure – Mix all ingredients except sweetener in the order listed, adding one kind at a time. Fill pie crust. Drizzle sweetener, if used, over filling. Place top crust on if called for; crimp edges together and slit top crust. Bake at 350 degrees for the time indicated, or until crust is browned and filling is soft and condensed.

Apple pie – 9-inch pie. Use rolled pie crust with top crust. Bake for 1 hour.

2 Tbsp. whole wheat pastry flour
½ tsp. cinnamon
¼ tsp. salt
½ tsp. grated lemon rind
4 cups apples, thinly sliced

Peach pie – 9-inch pie. Use rolled pie crust with top crust. Bake for 45 to 55 minutes.

4 Tbsp. whole wheat pastry flour
½ tsp. cinnamon
¼ tsp. salt
4 cups fresh peaches, thinly sliced
½ cup rice syrup or maple syrup

Sweet potato pie – 9-inch pie. Use pressed pie crust. Bake pie crust alone 15 minutes. Fill, garnish with pecans, and bake 20 minutes.

3 cups cooked sweet potatoes, mashed
1 to 1½ cups water
½ tsp. cinnamon
garnish: pecans

Squash and apple pie – 9-inch pie. Use rolled pie crust with top crust. Bake 45 to 55 minutes.

---

1 Tbsp. whole wheat pastry flour
½ tsp. cinnamon
⅛ tsp. salt
½ tsp. grated lemon rind
¼ cup raisins or currants
2 cups apples, thinly sliced
2 cups cooked winter squash, mashed

Comments – A 9-inch pie needs about 4 cups of filling. Filling can be fruit, vegetable, or a combination of fruit and vegetable.

When making fruit pies, flour mixed with salt and spice is used to thicken the liquid. Some fruits such as peaches and berries need more flour. Try fruit pies with any fruit desired: pears, strawberries, cherries, apples with strawberries, etc., using a small amount of sweetener if desired. Use a rolled pie crust with a top crust.

Vegetable pies can be made from cooked squash, sweet potatoes, or parsnips, singly or in combination. The cooked vegetables are mashed and mixed with liquid until soft but not runny. Filling will set while baking. Use a pressed or partially baked rolled pie crust for vegetable pies. A top crust is not needed.

When making combination vegetable and fruit pies, fruit is mixed with a flour mixture and then with the cooked mashed vegetables. Try other combinations: pear and squash, or apple and parsnip. Currants can be added for more sweetening. Use a rolled pie crust; a top crust is optional.

Pies can be made by setting a kanten gelled dessert in a completely baked crust. Bake any pie crust completely and cool. Make kanten dessert per recipe on page 168. Pour into shell when kanten has slightly cooled but has not set. Refrigerate to set. Try strawberry or creamy lemon kanten in pressed pie crust.

Granola

Procedure – Mix oil, salt, and sweetener. Heat if needed to make the mixture workable. Add ingredients, except dried fruit, in the order listed, one kind at a time. Mix well after each addition. Place in a 9″ x 13″ x 2″ baking pan. Bake at 350 degrees for 1 to 1½ hours, or until browned and crisp, stirring every 15 minutes. Remove from oven. Add dried fruit, if used.

Granola – Yield: 10 to 12 cups.

¼ cup corn oil
½ cup sweetener: rice, malt, or maple syrup
½ tsp. salt
¼ cup sesame seeds, washed and drained
½ cup sunflower seeds
8 to 10 cups rolled oats
½ cup currants or 1 cup raisins

Comments – It is easy to make many different kinds of granola by following the simple guideline of mixing oil, salt, and sweetener first, then adding ingredients one kind at a time with those of smallest measure first. Try adding cinnamon, vanilla extract, coconut, nuts, wheat or rye flakes, or other dried fruit such as apples.

Granola can be unsweetened, too. Use ½ cup water instead of the ½ cup sweetener, and follow basic procedure. Serve granola with water, grain milk (page 183), or purchased soymilk.

Popcorn

Procedure – Heat pan over medium heat. Add oil and heat until hot. Add popping corn and salt. Cover. Shake pan every 5 to 10 seconds. As corn starts to pop consistently, shake continually until all corn is popped, about 7 to 10 minutes.

Popcorn – Fills a 2 quart pan.

> 1 Tbsp. corn oil
> ½ cup popping corn
> pinch salt

Comments – Popcorn turns out best when the pan and oil are hot, so that corn pops quickly without absorbing oil. A stainless steel pan works well. The pan and oil each take 30 seconds to heat. A second batch will often pop quicker than the first batch, because the pan is completely hot. Salt brings out the flavor, but too much will hinder the popping. The salt will cook into the corn so you won't need to sprinkle salt on afterwards. If desired, sprinkle a small amount of soy sauce on hot popcorn; or roast some seeds, sprinkle them with soy sauce, and mix with popcorn.

Keep popping corn in the refrigerator and it will pop better.

Trail Mixes

Procedure – Roast seeds or nuts individually, page 127. While still hot, sprinkle with a small amount of soy sauce. Then mix all ingredients together.

Simple trail mix – Yield: 2 cups.

1 cup sunflower seeds
½ cup almonds
soy sauce, small amount
½ cup raisins or currants

Comments – Trail mixes are easy to make and can be made in great quantity to last during a long trip. Roast the seeds to make them more digestible, and use soy sauce to balance the fruit. Try adding other seeds or nuts, coconut, carob chips (add after nuts or seeds are completely cool), dried apples or apricots; in any desired proportions. Puffed cereal grains combine well with trail mixes also.

Beverages

Bancha Twig Tea

Procedure – Add tea to cold water. Bring to a boil. Simmer 15 to 20 minutes, then serve.

Bancha twig tea – Yield: 4 cups.

1 Tbsp. bancha twig tea
4 cups cold water

Comments – Bancha twig tea (or kukicha) is made from the roasted lower leaves and twigs of the tea bush. This tea contains only a trace of caffeine. Bancha twig tea is a soothing tea which can be served every day. A glass or enameled teapot makes the best tea. The twig tea can be used again. With each new pot, add 1 Tbsp. new tea for 4 to 5 cups cold water. When twigs accumulate to a ½-inch layer, discard. If you desire a milder tea, simmer 5 minutes, then steep 15 to 20 minutes before serving.

Grain Coffee and Tea

Procedure – To prepare grain, wash and drain 1 cup grain. Place in a dry skillet (no oil). Roast over medium to low heat until grain has popped, is very fragrant, and is turning dark brown, almost black. Stir often; after 30 minutes, stir continuously. It will take from 45 to 60 minutes to roast completely. For grain coffee, grind the hot roasted grain in a blender or a hand grain mill until it is powder. Cool. Store in a glass jar.

To make coffee or tea, add prepared grain to cold water. Bring to a boil. Simmer 15 to 20 minutes. Steep 10 minutes before serving.

Grain coffee – Yield: 5 cups.

> 2 Tbsp. grain powder
> 5 cups cold water

Grain tea – Yield: 5 cups.

> 2 Tbsp. whole grain
> 5 cups cold water

Comments – Grain tea is clear and light in color. Grain coffee is thicker and darker in color than grain tea. Both are available through stores, but when made at home, they are fresher. Use whole grains such as whole or pearled barley, whole wheat, brown rice, or a combination. It takes time to roast completely, but the roasted grain will keep over a year. Grain can be used a second time. Add 1 Tbsp. more grain for 5 cups water. After making tea, the whole grain can be cooked until soft and then eaten.

If you wish to purchase either grain coffee or tea, choose products which are free of dyes or commercial sweeteners. Use in the same proportion as listed above or follow directions on the package.

Grain Milk

Procedure – Cook grain in water until very soft. Cook rice by pressure cooking for 1½ to 2 hours, page 7. Cook rolled oats by simmering 45 minutes to 1 hour, page 12. Blend in blender until smooth, thinning if necessary. Strain if desired.

Grain milk – Yield: 5 to 6 cups.

1 cup brown rice or rolled oats; wash and drain rice before cooking
5 to 6 cups water

Comments – Grain milk is good over puffed cereals or granola. Serve hot or at room temperature. This milk will keep in the refrigerator for three to four days. If a sweet milk is desired, add ¼ cup currants or raisins and cook with the grain. This milk is not intended as a main source of food for an infant.

Juices, Hot

Procedure – Place all ingredients in a pan. Cover. Bring to a boil. Simmer 15 minutes over low heat. If using whole spices, strain when serving.

Small amount – Yield: 2 to 3 cups.

2 cups apple juice or apple juice blend
½ to 1 cup water
pinch salt
pinch ground cinnamon

Large amount – Yield: 20 cups.

1 gallon apple juice
1 quart water
½ tsp. salt
4 cinnamon sticks
¼ tsp. whole cloves

Comments – Hot juice is good during holiday times. Cooking with salt and spices makes a sweet blend. Try adding other juices, such as orange, apricot, or lemon.

Sparkling Juices, Cold

Procedure – Mix juices if using more than one kind. Add mineral water just before serving.

Small amount

2 parts juice
1 part mineral water

Large amount – Yield: 36 to 40 cups.

6 quarts juice (example: 1 gallon apple juice, 1 quart grape juice, 1 quart apple strawberry juice)
3 or 4 quarts mineral water

Comments – Sparkling cold juice is nice for summertime parties. Since carbonated mineral water loses its fizz after 20 minutes, add just before serving. Serve at room temperature or slightly chilled. Try any juice desired, such as orange juice, apple juice, apple with pear, grape, or apricot juice.

Mineral water may be served plain or with lemon or lime slices at room temperature, or slightly chilled.

Leftovers

Leftovers – The word "leftover" implies food which is merely reheated and served. But foods which are left over can be mixed together to form new dishes and meals. Sometimes, it is practical to cook extra so there will be intentional leftovers. Some dishes are very time consuming to make, but if some ingredients are already cooked, then the dish is simplified. For example, leftover cooked winter squash can be used as a filling for pie or muffins; medley salads or casseroles become easy when the grain or noodles are already cooked.

Ease of mixing – The more simple the leftover, the more versatile. Plain rice combines with more dishes than rice cooked with vegetables. A dish seasoned with just oil, salt, and soy sauce is easier to incorporate into a new dish than a dish with oil, salt, soy sauce, vegetables, and noodles.

Reheating leftovers – If leftovers have been refrigerated, reheat for better flavor. When food will be served in the same way, reheat by the following method: Place ½ to 1 inch of water in bottom of pan; lay leftovers on top; heat to boiling; simmer 3 to 4 minutes; mix. Rice and other grains heat through well without burning. Another way to heat leftovers is to place 1 inch of water in the bottom of a large pot. Place the whole pyrex or stainless steel bowl of leftovers into the pot. Cover. Steam 10 minutes. This method eliminates adding extra water to the dish.

Burgers

Procedure – Combine cooked grain and water. Mix to separate clumps of grain. Add other ingredients. Mixture should be firm. Heat oil in a skillet. Spoon mixture into the skillet. Flatten into burger shapes. Cover pan. Fry 7 minutes. Uncover, and fry other side 5 minutes.

Grain burgers – 8 three-inch patties.

1 cup cooked grain
1 cup water
½ small onion, finely minced; optional
1 cup whole wheat flour
1 Tbsp. corn oil for skillet

Grain burgers with miso – 8 three-inch patties.

1 cup cooked rice
1 cup water
1 Tbsp. miso
½ small onion, finely minced; optional
1 cup whole wheat flour
1 Tbsp. corn oil for skillet

Comments – Burgers are a perfect way to utilize cooked grain that is left over. Adding onions and/or miso makes them even more flavorful. Burgers can be made using any leftover grain, flour, or leftover noodle cooking water. Burgers can also be made with tofu, page 93.

Fried Grain Slices

Procedure – Scoop cooked cornmeal or creamed cereal into a loaf pan while it is still hot. Smooth the top of the loaf. Let stand until firm and completely cool. When ready to fry, turn the loaf out of the pan and slice it into ½-inch thick pieces. Heat oil in skillet. Pan-fry, uncovered, until browned, 3 to 5 minutes each side.

Fried grain slices

cooked and cooled cornmeal or creamed cereal
1 Tbsp. corn oil for skillet

Comments – Fried grain slices can be made from cornmeal or creamed cereals which have been boiled, sauteed and boiled, roasted and boiled, or sauteed and boiled with vegetables (see pages 12–17). It is good to plan ahead for making fried slices.

Casseroles

Procedure – Mix ingredients together, adding extra water or liquid if needed. Mixture should be moist yet hold its shape when placed into the baking pan. Place in an oiled pan. Cover, if desired, to prevent drying out. Bake 30 minutes at 350 degrees.

Casserole combination ideas

Cooked noodles, cooked tofu sauce, and fresh chopped scallions

Cooked rice, cooked layered vegetables, and cooked nut butter sauce

Cooked cornmeal, cooked beans, and fresh chopped scallions

Cooked noodles, cooked bechamel sauce, cooked fish, and fresh chopped scallions

Comments – Many casseroles are made of pre-cooked foods and a sauce. Leftovers are ideal ingredients in casseroles and can be mixed in any desired proportions. Generally, use grains, vegetables, and a sauce (or water). Casseroles can be made by layering leftovers into the pan rather than mixing. For example, place noodles in pan with steamed vegetables on top and bechamel sauce poured over.

Grain and Vegetable Pies

Procedure – Make rolled pie crust, page 174. Place bottom crust in pie tin. Mix filling. It should be moist and soft, yet not runny. Place filling into bottom crust. Place top crust on top of filling, if desired. Crimp bottom and top crust together and slit top crust to allow steam to escape. Bake 25 to 30 minutes at 350 degrees.

Grain and vegetable pie combination ideas

Cooked rice, cooked hijiki, water, and fresh chopped scallions

Cooked green vegetables, cooked cornmeal, and fresh beaten egg

Cooked vegetables, cooked fish, and cooked bechamel sauce

Cooked vegetables, cooked beans, and soy sauce

Comments – Pie fillings should be moist; they will set as they bake. Since there is a crust, use a higher proportion of vegetables to grain; or make a vegetable-only pie, mixing with beaten egg if desired.

Grain and Vegetable Porridges

Procedure – Place ingredients in a pot with water, soup, or liquid at bottom; firm or solid ingredients at top. Use at least the same amount of cooked grain as liquid. Cover. Bring to a boil. Simmer 15 minutes over low heat. Add soy sauce or miso to taste.

Grain and vegetable porridge ideas

Leftover miso soup, cooked rice, and fresh minced scallions

Leftover vegetable soup, cooked rice, and hard bread crusts

Water, cooked vegetables, and cooked noodles

Water, cooked vegetables, cooked beans, and cooked grain

Leftover vegetable soup, cooked noodles, and cooked fish

Comments – These thick, seasoned soups can be made with almost any leftovers. If leftover vegetables or noodles are big or long, cut into smaller sizes before making into porridge.

Ideas for Using Leftovers

Grains

Serve with roasted nuts, seeds, or a sauce.

Add to soup to heat through.

Mix with cooked vegetables. Cook vegetables by layering, page 29 or by steaming, page 44. During the last 5 minutes of cooking, layer grain on top to heat through.

Fry with vegetables. Saute or stir-fry vegetables, page 34. Add grain during last 5 minutes of cooking to heat through. Season.

Cook leftover grain into a new grain dish. Cook bulghur, cornmeal, or oatmeal with the usual amount of water, adding leftover cooked rice for the full cooking time.

Make into grain milk, page 183; porridge, page 192; casserole, page 190; pie, page 191; pancakes, page 155; pudding, page 165; salad, page 110; or bread, page 147.

Noodles

Serve with sauce or garnish.

Add to soup and heat through.

Make into salad, page 110; sea vegetable dish, page 71; casserole, page 190; or porridge, page 192.

Vegetables

Heat with cooked grain. Garnish with roasted seeds.

Add to soup.

Make into porridge, page 192; casserole, page 190; or pie, page 191.

Make into a dessert or topping, especially if winter squash, sweet potatoes, or parsnips. See page 176.

Soups

Serve over grain, noodles, or muffins.

Heat with cooked grain or noodles.

Thin soup and cook noodles or dumplings in it.

Make porridge, page 192.

Sea vegetables

Add soy sauce. Mix with cooked noodles or salad.

Make into a pie, page 191.

Beans

Serve with crackers, tortillas, or chips.

Heat with leftover grains or noodles.

Thin beans, add scallions and more seasoning, and serve over grain, noodles, biscuits, or muffins.

Thin beans to soup consistency and cook noodles, cornmeal, or dumplings in it.

Make into a spread or dip by pureeing in a blender and adding more seasoning.

Make into porridge, page 192; pie, page 191; or casserole, page 190.

Fish

Heat in soup.

Make into pie, page 191; or casserole, page 190, or grain burgers, page 188.

Salads

Add more of the seasoning that was in the original salad and mix with cooked noodles, grains, or sea vegetables.

Sauces

Serve over vegetables, grains, or noodles.

Serve as a spread or dip.

Make into pie, page 191; or casserole, page 190.

Pickles

Make less salty: Mince finely and mix with a small amount of lemon or ginger juice.

Mince finely and mix into salad or use as a topping for salad in the proportion of 1 part pickle to 4 parts salad. Let stand 15 to 20 minutes before serving.

Make into a condiment: Mince finely and mix with an equal part of minced raw cucumber or celery. Let stand 15 to 20 minutes before serving.

Breads

Serve in soup or with a sauce.

Steam dry or stale bread until soft, 10 to 15 minutes.

Make croutons: Cube bread. Fry in oil or toast without oil until crisp.

Fruit desserts

Use as a topping for pancakes or muffins.

Use as a filling in muffins or pie.

Use as an ingredient in pudding or cookies.

Theory

Yin and Yang

The macrobiotic "diet" – There are other diets which include brown rice and fresh vegetables. The macrobiotic diet is different in that it incorporates more than just food. There is a principle underlying the diet which helps us understand how food, among other things, affects our bodies and minds. This principle has been named "the order of the universe" by George Ohsawa, the modern-day founder of macrobiotics.

Definitions – The order of the universe means that everything happens in an orderly way. Planets, land forms, histories of peoples, sickness, health, emotions: all things follow a definable and recognizable order.

Yin and yang are the tools which help us to see this order and thus help us to create order in our lives. Yin represents expansiveness; yang represents contractiveness. These characteristics interact with each other to define all phenomena.

Yin and yang as descriptive words – Yin and yang are descriptive words to help classify and categorize. They are meaningful only when used to describe or compare things. Just as *light* and *heavy* are relative words, so *yin* and *yang* are also relative words. For example, wood is heavy compared with paper but light compared with rock. In the same way, vegetables are yang compared with fruit but yin compared with animal foods. Thus any thing can be either yin or yang depending on what it is compared with, or depending on the category.

Yin and yang and change – It is important to note that things themselves continually change, and the conditions acting upon things also change. What is yin at one time may be yang at another, depending on season, age, size, location of growth, etc.

Macrobiotic thinking is based on the idea that each person and each person's situation is unique due to a unique set of yin and yang factors, and that these factors are continually changing. Thus, it is preferable to learn the processes and procedures rather than memorizing sets of rules and lists of recipes.

Classifying yin and yang – The following examples of vegetable qualities are representative of the process of categorizing physical yin and yang factors.

Composition:

more yin	more yang
rich in potassium	rich in sodium
more watery	less watery (more dry)

Growth:

more yin	more yang
vertical growth above ground	vertical growth below ground
horizontal growth below ground	horizontal growth above ground

Size:

more yin	more yang
bigger	smaller
larger leaves	smaller leaves

Season and climate:

more yin	more yang
grown in summer	grown in winter
grown in warmer climate	grown in colder climate

Manner of production:

more yin	more yang
grown with chemical fertilizers	organically grown

Note that a carrot grown in a warmer climate is more yin than a carrot grown in a colder climate. However, such a "yin" carrot is still more yang than a tomato even if the tomato is grown in a colder climate because tomatoes as a category are much more yin than carrots, as shown in the next section.

Yin and yang and harmony – We experience yin and yang factors in our lives and then determine how to use other yang and yin factors to harmonize our present condition. For example, after eating something very salty, one becomes very thirsty. Once you have learned how to determine your own condition and situation, you can then use yin and yang to create and maintain harmony in your life. This can be done through many activities, one of which is eating.

Yin and yang and their importance to diet and cooking – We eat each day. As yin and yang factors change from day to day, our choice of food and preparations can harmonize these changing factors. When the situation changes again, the food and preparation also need to change. Cooking is a practical and daily way to apply yin and yang.

By following the simple guideline of "consume mostly grains and vegetables," you remain near the middle of the yin-yang spectrum. By eating mostly foods in the middle of the spectrum, it is easier to balance yin and yang.

Applying the theory of yin and yang to cooking – It is natural to follow the principle of yin and yang without a necessarily conscious decision. For example, when it is very cold, you desire warming things. And when it is very hot, you want cooling things. Simply observing yin and yang at work is a good way to begin understanding these principles.

To intentionally apply the principle of yin and yang, here are four general ideas to keep in mind.

- We need both yin and yang; the harmony of yin and yang is desired.
- It is easier to balance moderate yin and yang than extreme yin and yang.

- We become what we take in: If I eat mostly yin food, I become more yin.
- We can balance a situation by what we eat: I take in yin to balance a yang situation.

Yin and Yang of Foods and Preparations

Food categories – Foods can be categorized from yin to yang based on the ratio of yin and yang elements. The following spectrum gives a comparison of how food groups relate to each other in terms of yin and yang. This is only a general guide as many factors influence yin and yang characteristics. Each category may overlap one or more of its neighbors. For example, some vegetables are more yin than some beans.

more yin						more yang
oils	fruits	beans	vegetables	grains	animal foods	salt

Each food group can likewise be categorized from yin to yang.

Grains:

more yin							more yang
corn	oats	barley	brown rice	wheat	rye	millet	buckwheat

Vegetables:

more yin						more yang
tomato	cucumber	cabbage	squash	onion	turnip	carrot

Beans:

more yin				more yang
split peas	pinto beans	lentils	chickpeas	azuki beans

Food groups can be further categorized from more yin to more yang. This is a good way to learn the yin and yang of foods. Here's an example to get you started.

Root Vegetables:

more yin					more yang
red radish	turnip	daikon	rutabaga	carrot	burdock

Preparation categories – We can classify the methods of preparation as more yin or more yang. Again yin and yang are comparative words. Sauteed is yang compared with boiled but yin compared with baked.

more yin				more yang
raw	boiled	pressure cooked	sauteed	baked

Raw – Food that has not been altered by cooking or pickling.

Boiled – The water boils and steam goes up and out (expansion). Also included in this category are simmered, steamed, parboiled, and blanched.

Pressure cooked – Foods are subjected to higher pressure than normal atmospheric pressure. Foods become more condensed (yang).

Sauteed – The hot oil seals in nutrition and flavor (this factor is yang); but oil itself is yin because of its molecular structure. Also included in this category are stir-fried, pan-fried, and deep-fried.

Baked – Foods are surrounded by dry heat which condenses them. Also included in this category are roasted (top of stove or oven) and broiled.

Pickled – Foods are not cooked, but are changed through pressure, salt, and length of time. Thus the yin and yang qualities are also changed depending on the amounts of pressure and salt, and the length of time. Included in this category are all natural pickling methods.

Additional factors – Preparations in each general category change in their yin and yang relationships to each other as other conditions such as time, amount of salt, and amount of water change.

Time: more time is more yang.

more yin	more yang
3 day pickles	2 week pickles
vegetables baked 30 minutes	baked 1½ hours

Salt: more salt is more yang.

more yin	more yang
vegetables sauteed with a pinch of salt	sauteed with ½ tsp. salt
salad with no salt	salad with a dressing including soy sauce

Water: more water is more yin.

more yin	more yang
2 cups rice and 8 cups water	2 cups rice and 3½ cups water
pickles made in salt brine	pickles made by pressing with salt

---

Yin and Yang of Cooking

When cooking and planning meals, there are four basic ways of combining the various yin and yang factors of foods and preparations to create harmonized dishes and meals.

Food balancing food – Use yin foods and yang foods to balance each other. Avoid having many yin items or yang items without an appropriate balance, such as a meal with only fruit. Some examples of food balancing food are grains (more yang) and vegetables (more yin); fish (more yang) served with lemon (more yin); and sea vegetables (more yin) cooked with soy sauce (more yang).

Preparation balancing preparation – Use yin preparations and yang preparations to balance each other. Avoid meals with all items prepared in only one manner, such as a meal with all baked dishes. Use at least two preparations, such as pressure cooked food with sauteed food, or baked food and raw food.

Preparation balancing food – Use yin preparations for yang foods; yang preparations for yin foods. This method of balancing is particularly useful when preparing foods with strong yin or yang qualities, such as fruit, fish, or vegetables in the nightshade family. Some examples are baked fruit (yin food with yang preparation), or steamed fish (yang food with yin preparation).

Four-way balance – Most cooking falls into this category since this method incorporates the other three methods of balancing. It involves preparing a whole meal with balanced items. Some examples are pressure cooked rice (both yang) with simmered vegetables (both yin), baked fish (both yang) with raw salad (both yin), or boiled buckwheat (yin-yang) with sauteed cabbage (yang-yin).

Other Balance Considerations – While it is important to know how to balance various yins and yangs of foods and preparations, often there are other factors which must be balanced too. Sometimes, there is a specific situation, such as a health concern, which requires that the balance of foods and preparations be more yin or more yang. In addition to balancing all these factors, balancing acid and alkaline is also important.

The study of yin and yang can be a lifelong project. But you don't have to learn yin and yang in depth in order to cook good food. What is intended here is an introduction. Menu planning is very practical and a good place to start.

Menu Planning

This section is divided into areas of planning. Use this information as a guide in determining your own system of menu planning.

General plan – Menu planning is a way to organize yourself. You create a plan to establish order and consistency. There are four areas of planning outlined in this section: individual meals; daily; weekly; and seasonal. In actual practice they should be combined to work together.

I like to start with a weekly plan that takes into account seasonal needs. This might be written but more often merely thought through. Here is an example of a general weekly winter plan (only a few items are included): buckwheat sometime this week; lentil soup later in the week, perhaps Thursday; noodles on Friday; fish either Friday or Saturday.

Specific plan – While determining a general weekly plan, note which dishes require soaking or lengthy preparation, such as beans or bread. You can space the cooking so that major preparations fall on different days or plan to cook all these items on the same day.

Each day, think over the general plan and confirm or change it, depending on time, number of leftovers, and choice of fresh ingredients. Figure out each meal, and take into account daily needs. Note when to soak things and when to start cooking. To give an example, my general plan called for buckwheat sometime this week. On Tuesday night, noting there is only enough rice left over for breakfast, I plan buckwheat for lunch and a new pot of rice for dinner. I will wash the rice and put it on to soak about 9 a.m. Wednesday morning. On Wednesday night, knowing the general

204

plan is for lentil soup on Thursday, I plan to soak lentils after lunch on Thursday because they need only 2 to 3 hours of soaking.

Saving time – Planning ahead saves time in the long run. You know what to do ahead of time and what to purchase. Another way to save time is to let time work for you. Soak rice overnight and pressure cook it early in the morning before going to work. Knead bread in the evening and let it rise overnight; bake it in the morning.

Quantity – Another way to save time is to cook in quantity, especially those dishes which take a long time to prepare, such as bread, beans, pressure cooked grain, and pickles. If you are cooking for yourself only or are a light eater, you may be cooking in quantity already. Some vegetables, like winter squash, are usable as leftovers but most vegetables are best when freshly cooked.

Cooking in quantity allows meals to be coordinated. For example, cook cornmeal one day and have fried cornmeal slices the next day. Cook extra noodles and then make a salad. Cook extra winter squash and make filled muffins.

Individual Meal Planning

The three category system – One common plan shown in many macrobiotic books is the standard macrobiotic "pie." Percentages of various food groups are shown in the form of wedges of the pie: 50 to 60 percent whole cereal grains; 25 to 30 percent vegetables; 10 to 15 percent beans and sea vegetables; 5 percent soup; and 5 to 10 percent fish, fruit, and nuts.

I like to use this pie in a simplified form with only three wedges: grains, vegetables, and a combination of everything else. When planning meals, I try to include at least one item from each of these three categories. This can be three dishes, more than three dishes, or one dish with at least three things in it. Grains and vegetables combined make up the bulk of my meals and "everything else" is the smaller part. Sometimes I plan more grains and sometimes more vegetables. Sometimes "everything else" is very small; other times it approaches one-third of the menu.

So what is the "everything else?" – Anything that is not in the grain or vegetable categories. It can be soup, a sea vegetable dish, a condiment of roasted seeds or sea vegetables, pickles, fish, sauce, or a combination of these things. When preparing a meal with many different dishes, it is easy to incorporate items from the three categories. But when preparing a simple meal of grains and vegetables, this third item really makes a difference.

It often helps to choose grain first, vegetables (and soup if served) second, and side dishes and condiments third. If you are planning a bigger meal with fish or a special casserole, plan that first and let it be complemented by the choices of grains and vegetables.

Considerations for every meal

Salt – Cook salt into dishes rather than sprinkling it on food after it has been cooked. Salt changes as it cooks and is easier for the body to assimilate. Cook at least 20 minutes. Use soy sauce or miso in place of or with salt if desired. In this last case, the amount of salt can be reduced.

Oil – Use oil in at least one dish, or include seeds, nuts, or their butters. Adjust the amount of oil for your own needs.

Pickles and tea – Pickles and tea may be served at each meal if desired. Pickles aid digestion, and tea is soothing after eating.

Foods and preparations – Use a variety of preparations and foods to create balanced menus. For example, avoid baking everything or serving 100 percent grain.

Fancy and simple – Serve only one fancy dish such as a dish with many ingredients or colors. Simplify the rest of the meal.

Shapes – A variety of cutting styles makes the meal more attractive, both overall and within each dish.

Textures – A variety of textures makes the meal more appealing: creamy soups and sauces; chewy bread; firm vegetables; and crisp seeds and salads.

Colors – A spectrum of color is available: for examples; green, orange or yellow vegetables; black sea vegetables; red, green, or white beans; brown or tan grain. Colors can be used creatively over the whole meal as well as in each dish.

Daily Planning

Number and type of meals – Eating on a consistent schedule can create order and regularity. I like to eat three times a day with a light breakfast, simple lunch, and a fancier dinner. While you may desire a different daily plan, try to have one meal more elaborate than the others.

When beginning macrobiotics, all my meals were simple. My diet quickly became boring. When I studied cooking in macrobiotic classes, all my meals were gourmet-style and fancy. Then, my diet became too rich, and cooking, too time-consuming. Now, I aim for the middle: One meal each day is bigger and more elaborate than the others.

Daily needs – The United States government suggests a recommended daily allowance (RDA) for the general population which outlines the nutrients an individual needs each day. However, these allowances are standardized in such a way that individuals within large groups are considered to have the same needs. Foods commonly used within a macrobiotic diet supply these daily needs, but the macrobiotic approach allows that individual needs change as conditions change.

In planning menus, I like to draw up a minimum daily guideline per person. The following list is based on my current general needs; foods should be added or deleted depending on each person's needs and preferences. For example, when I was pregnant, I tried to have two daily servings of sea vegetables.

Miso soup – 1 serving
Another soup (not miso soup) – 1 serving
Grain – at least 2 servings
Noodles, bread, or a different grain – 1 serving
Sea vegetable – 1 serving
Dish with oil – 1 serving
Green vegetable – 1 serving
Yellow vegetable – 1 serving
Root vegetable – 1 serving
Leafy vegetable – 1 serving
Pickles – 2 servings
Tea – 2 servings

Weekly Planning

Cooking schedule – When working, it is necessary to set up a compatible cooking schedule. While working 8:00 to 5:00, Monday through Friday, I often cooked a lot on Saturday and Sunday, had leftovers on Monday and Tuesday, and made simple, quick meals on Wednesday, Thursday, and Friday. Now I am home and cook each day. Even so, I try to plan menus so two or more hours are spent in the kitchen for one meal only every second or third day. The rest of the time it takes only about one hour to prepare each meal, sometimes considerably less.

To simplify planning, you might have a special meal on the same night of each week: Thursday is noodle night, or Saturday is fish and dessert night. This simplifies planning.

Food variety – Grains and vegetables are served daily, yet they can be varied in the weekly schedule. For example, pressure cooked rice can be varied each time by mixing it with a different grain or with beans. Between pots of rice, boil other grains or noodles or make quick breads. Vary green vegetables during the week by using different kinds, such as cabbage, kale, and broccoli. Vary the dishes by using different preparations, such as layering, simmering, and stir-frying.

Weekly food guidelines – For foods that are not served daily, here are general weekly suggestions per person. As in the daily food guideline, this list can change depending on personal needs and preferences.

> Beans – 1 to 2 servings.
> Nuts, seeds, or sauce – 2 to 3 servings.
> Fish or egg – 1 serving each week in the winter;
>   1 serving every other week in the summer.
> Raw salad – 2 servings in the summer.
> Cooked salad – 1 serving in the winter.
> Dessert – 1 to 2 servings.

Seasonal Planning

Yin and yang of seasons – Summer is considered more yang (hotter) than winter, and summer menus should be more yin (cooler) than winter menus. Likewise, winter menus should be more yang than summer menus. Spring and fall are in the middle, so the menus are moderately yin and yang. Yet, spring menus can be slightly more yin because summer approaches, and fall menus can be slightly more yang because winter approaches. As seasons change, menus change both in the specific foods and the ways they are prepared.

Seasonal and local foods – Foods develop the qualities of the season and the location in which they grow. By eating local foods in their appropriate season, you eat the food which has adapted to that season and location, and thus you can more easily adapt to that season and location.

Seasonal variations in procedures – Any procedure can be used at any time of the year; you can pressure cook, saute, boil, bake, and pickle all year around. Yet for some dishes, certain procedures are more appropriate during a given season than others.

> Salad – Summer, raw. Winter, cooked.
> Miso soup – Summer, boiled. Winter, sauteed and
>   boiled.
> Pickles – Summer, brine pickles. Winter, pressed
>   pickles.

Of course, procedures may be chosen for reasons of balance or other considerations. You may wish to serve raw salad or fruit to balance turkey at Thanksgiving.

Other seasonal modifications – Amounts of salt, water, oil, and length of cooking time can be adjusted as the seasons change. For example, increase the proportion of water to rice in the summer and use a smaller proportion in the winter. Use less miso in miso soup in the summer and more in the winter.

Menus

This section includes food lists and several categories of sample menus. Beginning Menus includes familiar foods prepared in simple ways. Menus for Seven Consecutive Days shows a week's worth of meals and how to use leftovers.

Each item is followed by the page number of the recipe. Variations of recipes or procedures have been included in parentheses. An approximate time for preparation of each meal is noted under the last item. Soaking time and any required leftovers are also listed.

All menus may include storebought or homemade pickles. Bancha twig tea (page 181) may be served at any meal, also.

Menu Suggestions

Breakfast - Try a simple light breakfast of soup, if desired, and grain. Ideas for breakfast include:

> Miso soup.
> Soft cooked grain like oatmeal, rice, creamed cereals, etc., or
>   porridge of leftover grain.
> Topping for grain. Roasted seeds or sea vegetables or sesame
>   seed condiments.
> Breads, muffins, toast, pancakes, waffles.
> Spreads or sauces for breads.
> Granola and grain milk.
> Egg dishes.
> Tea.

Lunch or supper - Ideas for a simple meal of grain, vegetable, and one other dish include:

> Any grain dish.
> Any vegetable dish or grain and vegetable combination.
> Simple vegetable soup or miso soup if not served at
>   breakfast.
> Sea vegetable dishes.
> Condiments of roasted sea vegetables or seeds.
> Bread, toast, muffins, spreads, etc.
> Bran pickles.
> Simple salads or noodle dishes.
> Tea.

Dinner - For the largest meal of the day, add soup, beans, or whatever else is desired to the basic menu of grain and vegetables. Ideas for dinner include:

> Any grain dish.
> Any vegetable dish or grain and vegetable combination.
> Noodle dishes.
> Fancy soups with dumplings, creamy ingredients, flour,
>   fish, etc.

Bean dishes.
Fish or egg dishes.
Rich sauces with nuts.
Pressed salads and pickles.
Pan-fried dishes.
Desserts.
Tea.

Good combinations – Any of these ideas can serve as a base on which to build a meal.

Rice with roasted seeds, azuki beans, or split peas.
Millet with chickpeas, lentils, or dulse.
Buckwheat with sesame butter sauce, scallions, lentils, nori, or tofu.
Oatmeal with roasted sunflower seeds or dulse.
Cornmeal or corn bread with pinto beans, black beans, or lentils.
Bulghur with chickpeas or sesame butter sauce.
Creamed cereals with miso vegetables.
Udon or buckwheat noodles with clear kombu broths and garnishes.
Whole wheat noodles with nut butter sauce.

Quick and Easy Foods

Easiest foods to prepare - The following foods are the easiest ones from each food group. Note that some may be more involved than foods listed in other food groups. For example, it is easier to make salt brine pickles than bran pickles, but it is easier to make a salad than salt brine pickles.

Grains - Boiled grain; soaked, unsoaked using cold water, unsoaked using hot water.
Noodles - Noodles served with a sauce or cooked into soup.
Vegetables - Any vegetables simmered, layered, or baked.
Salads - Raw salads and mixed dressings.
Soups - Stews, boiled vegetable soups.
Beans - Boiled bean dishes.
Sea vegetables - Kombu used in bean dishes, agar-agar used in kanten gelled desserts.
Sauces and condiments - Nut butter sauces, spreads. Nuts or seeds roasted on top of the stove.
Pickles and pressed salads - Salt brine pickles. Salt brine pressed salads.
Fish and egg - Baked or broiled fish. Scrambled eggs.
Breads - Batter breads, muffins, biscuits, pancakes, dumplings.
Desserts and snacks - Fruit sauces, stewed dried fruit, grain puddings, drop cookies. Granola, popcorn, trail mixes.
Beverages - Bancha twig tea, juices.
Leftovers - Burgers, porridge.

Foods that can be prepared in small quantities - The following foods are the easiest from each food group to make in a small amount. These are especially useful when cooking for one.

Grains - Millet, oatmeal, cornmeal, bulghur, rice cream, hard-kernelled grains (rice, oats, wheat) in a small pressure cooker.
Noodles - All noodles.
Vegetables - All vegetables.
Salads - All salads.

Soups – Boiled vegetable soups, sauteed vegetable soups, kombu soups, instant soups.

Beans – Tofu, tempeh, lentils, azuki beans, split peas.

Sea vegetables – Roasted dulse, wakame, or nori.

Sauces and condiments – Mixed sauces, clear sauces, nut butter sauces. Nuts and seeds roasted on top of the stove.

Pickles and pressed salads – Pressed salads with salt brine or soy sauce brine.

Fish and egg – Pan-fried, broiled, or steamed fish. Scrambled eggs.

Breads – Pancakes, biscuits, muffins.

Desserts and snacks – Sauteed fruit, fruit in clear sauce, fruit with sauce, couscous puddings. Popcorn, trail mixes.

Beverages – All beverages.

Leftovers – Burgers.

Quickest foods to prepare – These foods can be prepared in 30 minutes or less. Use these ideas when in a hurry or when unexpected guests arrive.

Grains – Boiled millet, oatmeal, bulghur, cornmeal, couscous.

Noodles – All noodles.

Vegetables – Pressure cooked, stir-fried, sauteed with or without water, layered, or simmered vegetables. Some vegetables such as greens require more time to wash and some cuts, for example, dicing, take more time.

Salads – All salads and dressings.

Soups – Boiled soups, pressure cooked soups, instant soups, kombu soups.

Beans – Tofu, tempeh dishes.

Sea vegetables – Dulse or wakame salads. Roasted nori, dulse, or wakame.

Sauces and condiments – Mixed sauces, clear sauces, nut butter sauces, miso sauces, tofu sauces. Nuts and seeds roasted on top of the stove or in the oven.

Fish and egg – All except baked fish with vegetables.

Breads – Dumplings, pancakes, waffles.

Desserts and snacks – Sauteed fruit, fruit in clear sauce, fruit with sauce, couscous puddings. Popcorn, trail mixes.

Beverages – Bancha twig tea, juices.

Leftovers – Burgers, porridge, fried grain slices, most suggestions listed on pages 193-195.

Beginning Menus

Boiled oatmeal, page 12.
Simmered broccoli, page 44.
Roasted sunflower seeds, page 127.
Time: 45 minutes.

Split pea soup, page 88.
Boiled sauteed bulghur, page 16.
Simmered carrots, page 42.
Oat crisp, page 154.
Time: 1½ hours. Requires soaking peas 2 to 3 hours.

Celery and cabbage soup with noodles, page 56.
Boiled millet, page 11.
Winter squash and carrots, page 29.
Roasted almonds with soy sauce, page 127 (and comments).
Applesauce, page 162.
Time: 60 minutes.

Vegetable stew with kombu knots, page 48.
Boiled brown rice, page 10.
Cornmeal biscuits, page 153.
Nut butter and soy sauce gravy (use sesame butter),
    page 122.
Time: 1½ hours.

Celery, cabbage, and carrot soup, page 50.
Whole wheat noodles, page 23.
    Serve cooked noodles in soup.
Baked winter squash, page 28.
Time: 1½ hours.

Quick Menus

Whole wheat noodles, page 23.
Simmered broccoli and carrots, page 42 (variation).
Tofu and umeboshi sauce, page 125; or nut butter and soy
    sauce gravy (use sesame butter), page 122.
    Serve desired sauce on top of noodles and vegetables.
Time: 30 minutes.

Boiled bulghur, page 12; or reheated leftover rice (see
    reheating leftovers, page 187).
Butternut squash and kale, page 34.
    Serve vegetables over bulghur or rice.
Sauteed apples, page 160.
Time: 30 minutes.

Pan-fried tempeh, page 95.
Whole wheat bread, page 147, or storebought bread.
Pressed cabbage pickles, page 140, or storebought sauerkraut.
    Make a sandwich of tempeh, bread, pickles, and lettuce
    and sprouts as desired.
Couscous and squash pudding, page 167.
Time: 30 minutes. Requires leftover winter squash for
    pudding. Bread and pickles storebought or already made.

Tofu, carrot, and scallion soup, page 47.
Grain burgers (use brown rice), page 188.
Lettuce, cucumber, and radish salad, page 112.
Soy sauce dressing (use lemon juice), page 115.
    Serve dressing separately for use on salad.
Time: 30 minutes. Requires leftover rice for burgers.

Soba or udon noodles, page 23.
Medium or thin clear sauce, page 120.
Nori matchsticks, page 78.
    Serve sauce over noodles and garnish with nori.
Turnips, rutabagas, and carrots, page 32.
Time: 30 minutes.

Summer Menus

Creamy corn and green bean soup, page 60.
Rice salad, page 110.
Peach and apple kanten, page 168.
Time: 45 minutes. Requires leftover rice for salad.

Arame with green beans and carrots, page 72.
Whole wheat ribbon noodles, page 23.
    Mix noodles with arame, see comments under hijiki,
    page 71.
Corn on the cob, page 44.
Tossed lettuce, celery, and radish salad, page 114 (variation).
Umeboshi and scallion dressing, page 117.
    Mix dressing and toss with salad.
Time: 45 minutes.

Creamy cauliflower soup with dumplings, page 52.
Brown rice combination with barley, page 7 (variation).
Summer squash, page 38.
Lettuce, cucumber, and scallion pressed salad, page 138.
Time: 60 to 75 minutes. Requires soaking rice and barley for
    4 to 5 hours and pressing salad for 1 to 2 hours.

Black turtle bean soup, page 89.
Boiled brown rice, page 10.
Cornmeal batter bread, page 149.
Cucumber and avocado salad, page 114.
Time: 2 hours. Requires soaking beans for 6 to 8 hours and
    letting the bread rise in the sun for 3 to 4 hours.

Kombu clear soup with tofu and scallions, page 67.
Steamed cod, page 102.
Millet with vegetables, page 18.
Green bean salad with almonds, page 106.
Cantaloupe with sauce, page 164.
Time: 45 minutes.

Winter Menus

Bok choy, carrot, wakame, and millet miso soup, page 64
(see comments).
Buckwheat muffins, page 152.
Nut butter and soy sauce spread, page 130 (use sesame but-
ter and add minced scallions, see comments).
Time: 60 minutes.

Brown rice combination with whole oats, page 7.
Rutabagas, page 40.
Broccoli, page 36.
Time: 60 to 75 minutes. Requires soaking rice for 6 to 8
hours.

Creamy squash soup, page 55.
Boiled roasted buckwheat, page 14.
Cabbage, page 38.
Oatmeal and walnut cookies, page 171.
Time: 60 minutes.

Lentil soup, page 84.
Fried cornmeal slices, page 189.
Pressure cooked rice, optional, page 7.
Kale, page 42.
Onion or scallion miso, page 41.
Time: 2 hours. Requires cooked cornmeal; soaking lentils for
2 to 3 hours; and soaking rice, if used, for 6 to 8 hours.

Kombu clear soup with lemon, page 66 (see comments).
Baked brown rice, page 19.
Pan-fried perch, page 98; or broiled salmon, page 99.
Dulse with potatoes, page 73.
Brussels sprouts, cauliflower, and carrots, page 30.
Apricot pudding, page 165.
Time: 75 to 90 minutes.

Menus for Seven Consecutive Days

These menus are included as an example of an actual week's menus. They show how to use leftovers, how to use cooking time efficiently and economically, and how to provide variety. For reheating leftovers, see page 187. Note that quantities of some dishes are prepared for more than one meal. The number of meals' worth of each dish is indicated following the page number.

All menus may include storebought or homemade pickles. Bancha twig tea (page 181) may be served at any meal, also.

Sunday breakfast

> Roasted boiled oatmeal, page 15 – for 2 meals.
> Thick miso sauce, page 124.
> Time: 45 minutes. Soak rice, page 7 – for 5 meals.

Sunday lunch

> Pressure cooked brown rice, page 7.
> Hijiki with tempeh, page 71 – for 2 meals.
> Stir-fried yellow squash, cabbage, and carrots, page 34.
> Time: 60 minutes.

Sunday dinner

> Rice (from Sunday lunch).
> Creamy leek soup, page 61 – for 2 meals.
> Mustard greens, page 38.
> Baked apples with topping, page 159 – for 2 meals.
> Time: 60 minutes.

Monday breakfast

> Daikon, watercress, and nori miso soup, page 47.
> Oatmeal (from Sunday breakfast).
> Time: 10 minutes.

Monday lunch

> Rice (from Sunday lunch).
> Hijiki and tempeh (from Sunday lunch).
> Broccoli, page 36.
> Time: 30 minutes.

Monday dinner

> Creamy leek soup (from Sunday dinner).
> Rice (from Sunday lunch).
> Pressure cooked vegetables: green beans, yellow squash, and
>   onions, page 33.
> Baked apples with topping (from Sunday dinner).
> Time: 10 minutes. Prepare pressed cabbage pickles,
>   page 140.

Tuesday breakfast

> Grain and vegetable porridge using scallions, leftover rice,
>   water, and fresh miso, page 192.
> Time: 10 minutes.

Tuesday lunch

> Boiled bulghur, page 11 – for 2 meals.
> Collard greens with cornmeal, page 31 – for 2 meals.
> Roasted sunflower seeds, page 127.
> Time: 30 to 45 minutes.

Tuesday dinner

> Squash, turnip, and wakame miso soup, page 65 – for
>   3 meals. (See seasoning, page 46).
> Bulghur (from Tuesday lunch).
>   Add bulghur to miso soup.
> Whole wheat crackers, page 150 – for 2 meals.
> Cucumber, celery, walnut, and dulse salad, page 77.
> Time: 45 to 60 minutes. Soak rice and whole rye combina-
>   tion, page 7 – for 5 meals.

Wednesday breakfast

> Wakame miso soup (from Tuesday dinner).
> Crackers (from Tuesday dinner).
> Time: 5 minutes.

Wednesday lunch

> Pressure cooked rice with whole rye, page 7.
> Collard greens with cornmeal (from Tuesday lunch).
> Simmered carrots, page 42.
> Roasted nori or roasted dulse, page 78.
> Time: 60 minutes.

Wednesday dinner

> Rice and rye (from Wednesday lunch).
> Cabbage, carrot, and celery salad (any dressing), page 108 –
>   for 2 meals.
> Clear soup with scallions and soy sauce, using water from
>   cooked salad, see comments, page 107.
> Time: 60 minutes.

Thursday breakfast

> Wakame miso soup (from Tuesday dinner).
> Rice and rye (from Wednesday lunch).
> Time: 5 minutes. Soak chickpeas, page 90 – for 2 meals.

Thursday lunch

> Rice and rye (from Wednesday lunch).
> Roasted pumpkin seeds, page 127.
>   Serve seeds on rice.
> Cooked salad (from Wednesday dinner).
> Time: 10 minutes.

Thursday dinner

> Pressure cooked millet, page 8 – for 2 meals.
> Chickpea sauce, page 90 – for 2 meals.
>   Serve chickpea sauce over millet.
> Shredded lettuce with pressed cabbage pickles, page 195.
> Time: 2 hours.

Friday breakfast

> Daikon radish, scallion, and wakame miso soup, page 62 –
>   for 2 meals.
> Rice and rye (from Wednesday lunch).
> Time: 60 minutes.

Friday lunch

> Sauteed onion, celery, and carrots, page 36, with leftover
> millet cooked into the dish, see page 193.
> Nori with soy sauce, page 74.
> Time: 30 minutes.

Friday dinner

> Kombu clear soup with Chinese cabbage, tofu, and scallions,
> page 67 (variation).
> Pan-fried perch, page 98.
> Udon noodles, page 23.
> Serve soup over noodles and fish in one bowl.
> Winter squash, page 42.
> Time: 60 minutes. Soak rice, page 7 – for 2 meals. Knead
> whole wheat bread, page 147, and let rise overnight.

Saturday breakfast

> Wakame miso soup (from Friday breakfast).
> Buckwheat pancakes, page 155.
> Soy and ginger sauce, page 119.
> Time: 15 minutes. Bake bread for 1 to 1½ hours, page 147.

Saturday lunch

> Pressure cooked rice, page 7.
> Fresh bread.
> Walnut sauce with miso, page 123.
> Simmered broccoli, page 44 – for 2 meals.
> Time: 60 minutes.

Saturday dinner

> Chickpea soup using leftover chickpea sauce from Thursday
> dinner, see page 194.
> Rice (from Saturday lunch).
> Serve soup over rice.
> Broccoli (from Saturday lunch).
> Whole wheat muffins with squash filling, see comments,
> page 152.
> Time: 45 minutes.

Kitchen Hints

Timetable

Time flow – After you plan what to serve, work in an orderly way.

Give yourself enough time to cook. Allow a comfortable margin. I count backward from when I want to serve the meal, but you may wish to count forward and approximate the serving time. See general timing which follows.

Put water on to heat when preparing dishes which require boiling water.

Determine which dish needs the longest time and start to prepare this dish first. Assuming grains and beans have already been soaked, count the actual cooking time, and include preparation time for vegetables, soaking time for sea vegetables, standing times for grain (pressure cooker returning to normal pressure; standing time allowing bottom grain to lift off pan), and cooling time for quick breads.

Cook quicker dishes last so the whole meal is done at the same time.

Start tea when meal is served, so it simmers and steeps as you eat and will be hot when you are ready to serve it.

General timing – In order to have everything prepared by a certain time, I estimate the time required to prepare a meal based on four major categories as listed below. Note: I pressure cook beans

224

and hard-kernelled grains. If you boil these items, the time would be longer. Also allow more time if you cut vegetables slowly.

At least 2 hours – Preparing a whole meal which includes pressure cooked beans and/or hard-kernelled grains (assuming both beans and grains have been soaked).

At least 1 hour – Preparing a whole meal which includes thin-kernelled grains or grains that are cut, rolled, creamed, etc. Also meals with soups and/or sea vegetable dishes.

At least 30 minutes – Preparing noodles, incorporating or mixing leftovers into a new dish (like rice salad), pressure cooking soup or vegetables.

At least 10 minutes – Reheating leftovers.

I often prepare these foods at times when I'm not preparing a meal.

Breads – Let rise 2 to 24 hours.
Pickles – Ferment 2 to 4 days.
Soaking beans and grains – Soak for 2 to 8 hours.
Sesame seed condiments – Require 1 hour preparation time.

Cooking Hints

Top of stove or in the oven – Cooking on the top of the stove uses less energy than cooking in the oven because a smaller area is heated. When preparing a small amount of food, use the top of the stove. Roast seeds and nuts, heat leftovers, and toast bread in a skillet. Heat storebought or homemade mochi in a covered skillet over a low flame. Use the oven when baking breads, vegetables, or desserts, or when preparing many foods at the same time to make the maximum use of the space and the heat generated.

Boiling water – Put water on to heat as the first thing when

entering the kitchen to cook. It will then be hot when needed, and
will save time when bringing the dish to a boil. When adding boiling
water to a hot pan, add slowly and gently to avoid scalds. Pour away
from yourself. When adding water to a pan which has layered food,
pour water slowly over a spoon to avoid disturbing the layers.

Heat – Use the appropriate heat for the pan and the specific dish.
Higher heat cooks food quicker than lower heat, but is hard on the
pans and can burn the food. Use:

> *High heat* for short cooking times. Use at the beginning of
> cooking to heat up the pan or to bring food to the cooking
> temperature.

> *Medium-high to medium heat* to bring food to a good cook-
> ing temperature. Medium-high is preferable to high be-
> cause it is more gentle for pans.

> *Medium-low to low heat* once the pan is hot and the food is
> cooking well. Low heat can be used to keep food sim-
> mering for the remainder of the cooking time.

Very low heat for long cooking times of over 1½ hours. Usually used with a flame tamer.

Use of cover – Covers are used on pans for most cooking. Use a cover to hold the heat and steam inside, and thus cook the food faster. Use a cover to control spatters when pan-frying in oil. After cooking, use a cover on top of the pan to condense the steam and help lift food off the bottom of the pan. When all the food has been removed, soak pan with 1-inch of water and a cover on top to help make the pan easier to clean (especially if scorched).

Leave the cover ajar to help prevent spillover when cooking noodles, beans, or other foamy foods. Remove the cover near the end of cooking for some sauteed dishes or sauces to help evaporate extra water. Lift the back edge of pot covers first so the steam goes away from you, and thus avoid steam burns.

Preparing to Saute – Heat the pan over medium heat before adding oil. Stainless steel pans heat in 15 to 30 seconds; cast iron and enameled ware heat in 1 to 2 minutes. Add oil to the heated pan and heat the oil for 15 to 30 seconds before adding vegetables so vegetables will cook quickly and not just absorb oil.

Sauteing Vegetables – Vegetables are added to heated oil in a hot pan one kind at a time, usually beginning with onions. Saute the onion until the color changes, that is, the opaque white color changes to a transparent color. The time required for this change varies with the size of the pan and the number of onions. One onion may become transparent in 1 to 2 minutes while 5 onions may take 5 to 7 minutes. Add other vegetables and saute until the color changes or the vegetables begin to condense.

Serving proportions – When serving, follow the suggestions in the individual meal planning section, page 206. Use the standard recommendations as a guideline for how much to serve of each dish in relation to the others. Proportions can change. You may wish to include more grain per vegetables or more vegetables per grain. You may wish to make 95 percent of the meal grains and vegetables with 5 percent seeds; or 70 percent of the meal grains and vegetables and 30 percent of the meal beans, salad, dessert, or other items.

Approximate sizes of first servings for a meal including rice, vegetables, seeds, soup, pickles, and tea are shown in the following list.

> Rice – 1 to 1½ cups
> Vegetables – ¾ to 1 cup
> Roasted seeds – 2 Tbsp.
> Soup – 1½ cups
> Pickles – 1 Tbsp.
> Tea – 4 oz.

Examples of servings of other items are:

> Dry condiment – 2 tsp.
> Bean dish – ½ to ¾ cup
> Noodles – 1½ cups
> Sea vegetable dish – ¼ cup
> Bread – 2 slices
> Fish – 2 to 4 oz.
> Dessert – ⅛ of a 9-inch pie or ½ cup applesauce

When serving each plate, make it look attractive by arranging foods so that the colors are most enhanced. Use garnishes to add flavor and color. Tan grain with a tan sauce looks more appealing when parsley is sprinkled on top. Fried fish served on a plate looks inviting when lemon half-rounds or sprigs of parsley accompany it.

Buying Food

Buy foods you will use. Don't force yourself to buy rye flakes, for example, if you wouldn't use them. Try to buy the best quality you can find, such as whole, unpolished, organically grown, and free from preservatives. Buy seasonal vegetables whenever possible, locally grown if available. Flours should be freshly ground and tofu and tempeh freshly made.

Buy undyed, untoasted sea vegetables. Fertile eggs from free-ranging birds are preferred. Buy cold pressed oils; commercial production uses chemicals to extract and refine the oil. Unrefined oils are pressed without further processing and are preferred.

Buy unrefined, mineral sea salt. Use unpasteurized and aged soy sauce and miso; pasteurization kills beneficial bacteria. Buy undyed umeboshi with no preservatives added. Bancha twig tea should be roasted and made from older twigs and leaves.

First time shopping list – If you are starting from scratch, use this list as a guideline. The vegetables on this list will feed 2 people for 2 to 3 days; the grains will feed 2 people for 6 to 8 days.

    2 pounds short grain brown rice
    1 pound rolled oats
    1 pound millet
    1 pound whole wheat macaroni
    1 pound lentils or split peas
    ½ pound almonds or sunflower seeds
    1 bottle sesame oil
    1 bottle soy sauce
    1 package two-year-old barley miso

4 ounces unrefined sea salt
1 package bancha twig tea
1 package kombu sea vegetable
1 jar sesame butter
4 onions
1 to 2 pounds carrots
1 medium cabbage
1 bunch celery
1 bunch broccoli
1 medium butternut squash or 1 pound yellow squash
4 apples

Storing Food

Grains, flours, beans, seeds (uncooked) – Keep in airtight covered containers in a cool place at room temperature. They can be refrigerated for long storage or if in a hot climate. Place bay leaves in the containers to discourage bugs. Use flours within a week of purchase or grinding; they lose flavor and nutritional value as they sit. Use seeds within 2 months as they can become rancid. Grains and beans will keep 6 to 8 months.

Vegetables and fruits – Keep vegetables in a cool place. Onions and winter squash will keep in a cellar if whole and free from any cuts or bruises. Store squash so they don't touch each other, and turn them occasionally. Most vegetables and fruits keep well in the refrigerator. If bunches have twist ties and bands, remove them before storing. If the vegetables are wet, allow them to dry before storing so they won't rot. Spread them on a paper bag and leave them at room temperature until dry.

Generally, roots keep longer than greens. Keep in vegetable crisper or plastic bag in the refrigerator and use while still crisp. If vegetables are placed in the refrigerator as is, they tend to dry out. Some vegetables such as lettuce, scallions, and mushrooms keep well in cotton bags. Others, like celery, do better in plastic or in an airtight container. Parsley keeps well standing in a jar of water in the refrigerator.

Tofu and tempeh – Keep in the refrigerator 7 to 10 days and cover tofu completely with water. Change water every other day. If the tofu smells bad, it has spoiled. Tempeh can be frozen for longer storage (use within 2 months).

Fish and eggs – Use fish within a day or two of purchase. Store on ice if desired. For longer storage, sprinkle lemon juice over fish and freeze. Eggs will keep in the refrigerator for 1 month. Keep in the carton.

Oils and nut butters – Keep in a cool, dark place to prevent rancidity. Refrigerate in hot weather or if not used within 1 month.

Salt, miso, soy sauce, and umeboshi – Keep salt in a dry place. It will keep for years. Natural sea salt has no additives and may cake. Keep miso in a cool place. Refrigerate for long storage. If a white mold forms on top, it shows that miso is unpasteurized. This mold can be mixed in or scraped off.

Keep soy sauce in glass in a cool place. If you buy a large quantity and keep it for a long time (like a gallon over a year), white flecks may float to the top. The flecks do not harm the soy sauce but show that the soy sauce is unpasteurized. The soy sauce can be strained and used. Keep umeboshi plums and paste in a cool, dry place. They will keep a long time; if kept over a year, they will dry somewhat and the salt may crystalize.

Sea vegetables, arrowroot, bancha tea, and herbs and spices – Keep in a dry place, avoiding a sunny window or a warm spot such as above the stove. Keep herbs and spices in covered containers and use within one year of purchase. Bancha twig tea and arrowroot (kuzu) will keep for over a year while sea vegetables will keep two or more years.

Cooked foods – Cooked foods will keep at a cool, room temperature until the next meal. Remove from cooking pans, place in bowls, and cover with a mat or basket so air can circulate but food won't dry out. If the container is tightly covered, the food may spoil.

Grains and tea will keep one to two days.

When refrigerating, cool foods to room temperature before placing in the refrigerator. Keep in covered containers to prevent drying out and absorbing smells. If using plastic containers, cool foods before putting them in plastic. Soup and tea keep well in glass jars.

Tools: Care and Use

Outfitting Your Kitchen

You may already have common kitchen tools such as pots and pans, bakeware, mixing bowls, and spoons. In addition to these, other tools are of great help.

Vegetable brush – Different types of natural bristle brushes are available. Some have a handle; some are held in the hand. Use only with clean water; avoid soap. Vegetable brushes can be used to clean bamboo mats and suribachi.

Knives – A rectangular Japanese knife is ideal for cutting vegetables as it is lightweight and gives a clean, crisp cut. Use a serrated knife for cutting bread. A small paring knife is handy for coring foods but slow when chopping on a board.

Pots and pans – Use stainless steel, cast iron, pyrex, ceramic, or enameled cookware. Aluminum cookware is not recommended as aluminum can react with food and leave traces of aluminum in the food.

Pressure cooker – This is a big investment, but it is well worth it because a pressure cooker can provide a lifetime of service. There are various kinds and sizes. Buy stainless steel or enameled ware rather than aluminum. Inquire about replacement parts when buying. Parts for some brands are hard to find.

Flame tamer – A flat metal disc with punched holes, it is placed between a pan and the burner to spread the heat and help keep the food from sticking to the bottom of the pan and burning. It works well with a pressure cooker.

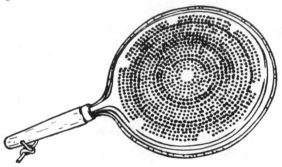

Soy sauce dispenser – There are different types of glass containers designed to dispense soy sauce drop by drop. Some soy sauce is sold in small dispensers. A glass screw-on cap will last longer than a plastic one.

Tea strainer – Strainers made of bamboo or ceramic are used to strain tea when serving. Clean with a vegetable brush and avoid soap.

Japanese grater – This kind of grater shreds the food very finely so that juice can be extracted from the shreds. Available in oriental food stores or through mail order, it may be of porcelain or metal.

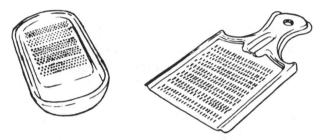

Miscellaneous items – These specialty items are useful: Suribachi and suricogi, Japanese mortar and pestle used to blend food; Japanese pickle press; Foley food mill; and hand or electric flour mill.

Pots and Pans

Heavy pans – Heavy pans have thick walls and bottoms. Often, they are made of cast iron, enameled cast iron, or enameled steel. Heavy pans take a longer time to heat than light pans, yet they hold the heat well and can be used for longer cooking times. Waterless cooked vegetables (sauteed in oil with salt) and dishes which require a long cooking time such as soups, grains, and beans cook well in heavy pans and will not be as likely to burn.

Light pans – Light pans have thin walls and bottoms. Often, they are stainless steel. Aluminum pans are light, but aluminum leaches into the food, so don't use them. Stainless steel pans heat quickly and are good when cooking dishes which require a short cooking time such as simmered vegetables, noodles, and quick soups. They tend to scorch if used for long cooking times, so place a flame tamer underneath.

Heat – High heat is hard on pans, especially over a period of time. Rather, use high or medium-high heat to reach a good cooking temperature, and then turn the heat to low to maintain that temperature.

Extreme temperature changes – Avoid exposing any pan or utensil to extreme changes of temperature. Avoid putting hot pans in dishwater until cooled. Avoid adding cold water to a hot pan. Use boiling water, or cool the pan first and then add cool water.

Burned pans – Slight scorches are easy to take care of. After the dish has finished cooking, remove the pot from the burner, but do not remove the food from the pot. Let the pot stand with the cover on for 10 to 15 minutes. The steam will condense and lift the food at the bottom so all the food can be mixed together. Grains respond especially well to this method and a slight scorch can even add flavor.

In the case of a badly burned pan, remove all food and discard any which is inedible. Soak the pan in cold water overnight with the cover on. Gently scrub off the burn the next day. If the burn is very stubborn, boil uncovered with 1-inch of water for 15 minutes; then soak covered overnight. If the burn still won't lift, let it wear off, and be careful with that pan.

To avoid burns, use lower heat, time carefully while simmering, cook in a pan appropriate for the dish, and use a flame tamer for long cooking times.

Cast Iron Ware

Seasoning – Non-enameled cast iron utensils must be seasoned to coat the metal so the pan can be used without rusting or imparting a metallic flavor. The initial seasoning takes 1 to 2 hours and can be repeated whenever desired. Cast iron pans improve with age.

Remove the wax finish from American-made pans before seasoning. Wash pan in hot soapy water, rinse well, and towel dry. If using a gas stove, place over a medium flame. If using an electric stove, place the pan in a 350 degree oven to heat. Heat until all the finish has smoked off; it will take 10 to 15 minutes (turn on a fan and open the doors). Cool 5 minutes. Coat inside and outside with a very thin coating of cooking oil. Place over flame or in the oven again, and heat to settle the oil into the pan. This will take 5 to 7 minutes; the pan may smoke. Cool. Coat the inside again. Heat another 5 to 7 minutes to settle the oil into the pan. The pan is then ready to use.

If the pan gives a metallic flavor after the initial seasoning, saute an onion in it and discard the onion. Wash the pan in hot soapy water, rinse well, heat, and oil. It is better to season a Dutch oven in an oven than on top of the stove. Heat and oil both the pan and the lid; however, don't put the lid on the pan while heating or they will seal together.

Washing and using – If the pan has been used for dry roasting or pan-frying in oil, you don't need to wash it. But if the pan has been used for vegetables or wet cooking, wash in clean water without soap, gently scrubbing with an abrasive pad. Heat over a burner or in the oven to dry completely. Coat lightly with oil if needed (especially during the first months of use).

Cast iron pans are ideal for sauteing vegetables, toasting nuts and seeds, dry roasting grain and flour, and pan-frying fish and burgers. If used for soups or watery dishes, the food may pick up a metallic flavor, especially if the pan is new.

Miscellaneous Kitchen Utensils

Enameled cookware – Be careful not to chip the enamel with metal implements or abrasive pads. Don't dry-roast grain, flour, nuts, or seeds in them since the dry heat may crack the enamel. Avoid extreme temperature changes; especially avoid adding cold water to a hot pan as this may crack the enamel.

Knives – Use a kitchen knife only for its intended purpose; don't pry up lids or cut paper, wood, string, etc. When cutting vegetables on a board, take care to cut only the vegetable, not the board, to help keep the knife sharp. When removing vegetables from the board, use the back of the knife to pick up vegetables or to push them off the board. Don't scrape the sharp edge of the blade across the board as this will dull the blade. After using a knife, wash and dry it immediately (don't soak it) and put it away in a knife rack or holder. A sharp knife works better and is safer to use than a dull one; sharpen as often as necessary by any desired method. After sharpening, wash the knife to remove any oil or particles of metal.

Cutting board – Hold the knife properly, and cut straight down to get a clean cut without needless cutting of the board. After using, clean the board by scrubbing both sides with a vegetable brush and clean water. Avoid soap as the board may absorb it. After cutting fish, rub lemon into the board to remove odors; then scrub with brush and clean water. Dry the board completely so it will not absorb water and become warped. To protect the board from cracking, rub cooking oil into it occasionally.

Wooden and bamboo utensils – Avoid soaking wooden utensils as they may swell and warp. Wash and rinse well. Oil occasionally to protect from cracking. Wash bamboo baskets, mats, and strainers if food gets stuck to them. Use vegetable brush and clean water. Avoid soap.

Using a Pressure Cooker

On first using a pressure cooker, I turned the flame down at the first noise out of fear that the cooker would blow up. The food was disappointing because the correct cooking pressure had never been reached. Later, when taking cooking classes, I learned how to use a pressure cooker to make really good tasting food, observing what was important for safe pressure cooking.

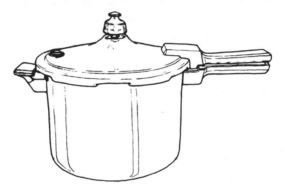

Cooking with pressure – A pressure cooker has an airtight seal, making possible a pressure inside the cooker greater than the atmospheric pressure outside the cooker. Foods cook quickly and condense from this strong pressure. Learning to use a pressure cooker well involves becoming familiar with your cooker and learning how to recognize full pressure.

Vent – The vent is on top of the cooker and holds the weight. It releases excess pressure and steam. It is important that it is always clear so the correct pressure will be maintained. If the vent clogs, pressure can build up, and the pressure relief plug may pop out. Here are safety tips for the vent. 1. Check hole before placing lid on cooker to make sure vent is clear. Insert a wire or a pipe cleaner to clean if needed. 2. Avoid pressure cooking foods which may block the vent when they cook, such as soybeans, split peas, rolled oats,

noodles, and fruit. 3. Soak foods that may cause blockage if unsoaked, such as whole oats, barley, and all beans. 4. Allow enough
cooking space. If the cooker is more than two-thirds full, food may
boil up into the vent. 5. While cooking at full pressure, tap the
weight occasionally (if it isn't already gently rocking) to make sure
some steam escapes. Steam signals that the vent is open.

Weight – The weight fits on top of the vent. It controls and maintains pressure. When the sealed cooker is being heated, the weight
keeps all the steam inside and the pressure increases. When up to
full pressure (15 lbs.), the steam and pressure are strong enough to
jiggle the weight. When the weight jiggles, some steam escapes along
with some pressure. Gentle rocking shows that there is full pressure,
and also that any excess pressure is being released.

Gasket – The gasket is a rubber ring which fits in the cover and
creates a tight seal so the cooker can reach full pressure. Before
putting the ring in the cover, make sure that both ring and cover are
clean of any particles. The ring may shrink or become hard in time
and should then be replaced. If the cooker doesn't reach full pressure, or if there is leakage from between the cover and the pot, you
may need a new ring.

Plug – The pressure relief plug is made of rubber and it (or some
other means of releasing pressure) is a safety device found on all
pressure cookers. It may be under or opposite the handle of the
cooker. If the pressure becomes too high (usually due to a clogged
vent), the plug is designed to pop out and release the pressure before
it becomes dangerously high. The plug may harden in time. If there
is leakage from the plug hole, the plug may need to be replaced. The
plug and the gasket are often replaced at the same time.

Bringing to full pressure – Place ingredients in the cooker. Check
the ring and fit it into the lid. Check the vent to make sure it is clear.
Lock the cover on the cooker. Place the weight on the vent. Place the
cooker over medium to medium-high heat. Pressure will increase.
When the pressure becomes stronger, the cooker will begin to make

noise which will increase with increased pressure. At full pressure (15 lbs.), the noise peaks, and the weight gently rocks. It will take 10 to 30 minutes to reach full pressure, depending on the quantity of food. Rocking of the weight and noise signal full pressure, not dangerous pressure (because steam escapes from the vent at the same time). Dangerous pressure is usually caused by a clogged vent.

Cooking at full pressure – When the cooker reaches full pressure, remove it from the heat. Place a flame tamer on the burner, and set the cooker on the flame tamer (if cooking vegetables or soup, omit the flame tamer and just turn down the heat). Turn the heat to low, but not so low as to let the pressure drop. Start timing. Maintain full pressure for the full cooking time, not allowing pressure to go up or down. Usually there is no strong steady noise after the peak, but the weight may rock and release some steam. Train your ear and eye to recognize your cooker's sign of full pressure. The secret of good pressure cooking is to get the cooker to full pressure and keep it there for the full cooking time. Steam signals that the vent is clear and is a good sign. The rocking weight signals that the cooker is still up to full pressure. If the weight isn't rocking, tap the weight; if there is some hissing and steaming, everything is fine. If there is no steam or noise and if the heat has been very low, the pressure has probably dropped. If 15 or more minutes of cooking time remain, turn up the heat to increase the pressure. If the flame has been high, see precautions below.

Precautions – While the cooker is at full pressure, it is important to stay nearby in case a high-pressure situation occurs. Take precaution if the cooker makes a peaking noise for a second time, signaling a too-high pressure. Remove the cooker from the burner for 3 to 4 minutes or until the weight rocks normally. Then return the cooker to the burner and set the heat lower.

Take precaution if the heat has been high and if, when tapping the weight, there is no noise or steam. This can signal that the vent is clogged or that there is not enough liquid in the cooker. Remove cooker from heat and run water over the lid until the pressure is reduced completely. Remove the weight and lid. Check the vent and clean it if it is clogged. Add liquid to the cooker if necessary. Return lid and weight. Continue cooking.

Leakage – If steam or foam escape from between the cover and pot, the seal is not tight. This may be caused by the cooker not being properly closed, food stuck to the gasket or to the top of the pot, or the gasket getting old and not fitting snugly. Reduce the pressure completely by running cold water over the lid. Remove the cover. Check the gasket and top of the pot for any stuck food, and clean if needed. Refit the gasket in the cover. Replace the cover, close completely, and resume cooking. If foam still comes out, the gasket does not fit snugly and should be replaced.

If foam comes out from the vent, the cooker may be too full. A little foam is not unusual, but if there is so much that it covers the lid completely, the vent may clog and create a problem. Watch carefully. If steam comes out with the foam, the vent is open. Beans often produce foam, as do unsoaked grains.

Removing the cover – Let the pressure drop completely before removing the weight and cover. Let stand until the pressure drops, or run cold water over the lid (especially when cooking vegetables). When there is no steam or noise when tapping the weight, remove the weight, and then the cover.

Cleaning and storing the cooker – Remove the gasket from the lid and wash separately. Clean the weight and the vent hole if dirty or clogged. When storing, keep the cover unlocked or inverted. If locked, the gasket may deform.

Safety rules

– Cook appropriate foods only. Avoid foods which may clog the cooker, and soak those which may clog the cooker if unsoaked.
– Fill cooker no more than two-thirds full.
– Check vent hole to make sure it is open before cooking. While cooking, keep in mind that the vent must be clear or the cooker may reach too high a pressure. Steam escaping from the vent signals that the vent is open.

- Pay attention while cooker is going up to pressure.
- Turn down the flame at the right time.
- Remove cover only when pressure is down and the weight is off.

Using a Suribachi

A suribachi is a ceramic bowl with unglazed grooves. A suricogi is a wooden pestle. Together, they resemble a mortar and pestle and are used to blend food. Suribachi come in various sizes. Use a size large enough so the ingredients do not spill as you grind.

Placement of the bowl – Place the bowl in one of three places: On the floor in a corner of the room, kneel and sit on your heels and wedge the bowl firmly into the corner with your knees; on your lap as you sit in a chair; or on a table at a good working height, the suribachi placed on a towel to avoid slipping.

Holding the suricogi – Hold suricogi (pestle) with both hands, one near the bottom and one near the top. The one near the bottom guides the suricogi all around the bowl, crushing and blending ingredients. The one near the top holds the top of the suricogi as still as possible.

Grinding – Vary the strength of grinding depending on the food being ground, and the placement of the bowl. Grind lightly when crushing seeds or mixing ingredients. Grind strongly when grinding salt or when making a fine mixture. It is easy to grind strongly when the bowl is on the floor and wedged into a corner.

Cleaning – An easy way to clean all those grooves is to pour hot water or broth around bowl to loosen clinging ingredients. Remove and add to soup. Then wash bowl in clean water with a vegetable brush; avoid soap.

Using a Knife

Rocking Method – Upon purchasing a rectangular vegetable knife, I began to cut vegetables following various cutting diagrams shown in cookbooks. I held the vegetables with fingers out. I held the knife loosely at the end of the handle and cut by rocking the knife, keeping the front of the knife on the board and using the back of the knife to cut. The cut used a down, back stroke. It took a long time to cut vegetables, and the pieces were uneven.

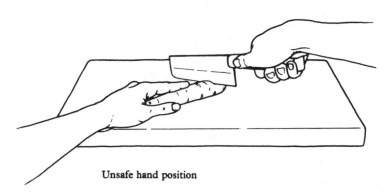

Unsafe hand position

Whole knife method – In cooking classes, Cornellia used a different method of cutting. She cut fast and very evenly. She held the vegetables with curled fingers, using the tips of the fingers and nails

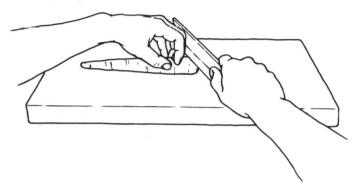

to keep the vegetables from moving. In this way, the upper part of the knife blade comes in contact with the knuckles, and the cutting edge is far from the fingertips. After each cut, the knuckles move back ever so slightly, measuring the distance of the next cut.

Cornellia held the knife differently, too. She held it firmly and grasped the knife at the junction where metal meets handle. This

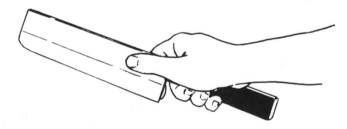

way of holding the knife allows more control when cutting. To cut, the whole knife is picked up, and then sliced down on a forward stroke. The upper arm and body move forward with this cut, and the blade meets the board evenly.

Learning this whole-knife cutting was awkward for me and gave me cramps for a few days. After ten days, it was comfortable; and in one month, I was cutting faster and more consistently. If you desire, learn this method by practicing slowly.

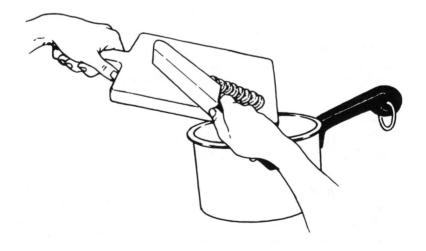

Cutting Vegetables

Cut vegetables cook faster than whole vegetables; smaller cuts cook faster than larger ones. Cutting allows different vegetables to be combined in the same dish so they can cook in the same time. Cutting allows the cook to be creative. Variation in the cutting styles makes each dish and the whole meal more attractive.

Using vegetables – Generally, younger vegetables are more tender than older vegetables. Also, smaller vegetables are more tender than larger ones. Use tender vegetables in salads, or in dishes which cook in a short time. Use older and larger vegetables in dishes which require longer cooking times such as soups, beans, or vegetable dishes. Some vegetables such as celery and greens come in bunches with both small and large pieces. Separate small and large pieces for various uses; small tender pieces of celery in salads, large pieces in soups.

Sizes and shapes of cuts – Use larger cuts for stews which simmer an hour or longer and for vegetables which will be served alone as a side dish, like winter squash. Young tender vegetables, which cook quickly, should be cut in large pieces to prevent them from becoming overcooked and mushy.

Use smaller cuts for most soups, grain dishes, and vegetable combination dishes. Larger, older vegetables will cook more thoroughly if cut in small pieces.

Use a different cut for each vegetable in a dish. Don't use all rounds or all dice cuts, but allow the cuts to complement one another. Matchsticks and crescents go well together, as do mince and quarter-rounds. Rounds and matchsticks look awkward together,

247

but large crescents and logs look appealing. Vary cuts for different vegetables used in the same meal. Use both large cuts and small cuts; similar large pieces for a side dish and similar small pieces for soup.

When cutting, notice that some vegetables require different cuts for different parts: The stems of greens are often cut into thin rounds, while the leaves are often cut into squares; broccoli flowers and stems are cut differently. Some vegetables vary in their dimensions: A carrot is wider at the top than the bottom. When cutting into quarter rounds, cut the top into thinner cross cuts and the bottom into thicker cross cuts so all pieces will cook evenly. Celery varies in that the inside stalks are more tender and can be cut into larger pieces while the outside stalks are more tough and are best cut into thinner or smaller pieces. Bunched vegetables such as scallions vary in size: Cut smaller scallions into larger sizes and larger scallions into smaller sizes when used in the same dish.

Cutting protocol – Cut one kind of vegetable at a time. Remove from board into a bowl until ready to cook, or cut vegetables in the order of use and put them directly into the pot. Wipe the board and knife with a clean sponge (no soap) between different kinds of vegetables, especially for vegetables used in different dishes. Flavors can mingle on the board, and strongly flavored vegetables like onion and garlic can change the flavor of another vegetable.

For use of knife, see page 244.

Cutting Styles

Minced onions

1. Slice onion in half lengthwise.
2. Place one half on board, cut side down, root end farthest from knife.
3. Slice into the onion, leaving onion together at root. Leave just enough to keep onion together. This connection makes the next step easier.

4. Slice across the cuts.
5. When you get to the uncut part, cut as necessary in order to mince.
Note: Cuts can be closer together for fine mince or farther apart for large mince.

Crescents

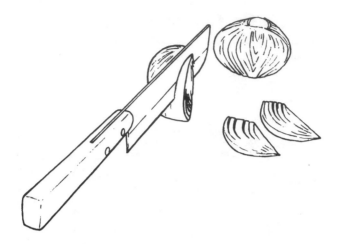

1. Slice vegetable in half lengthwise.
2. Hold one half with cut side away and root up.
3. Slice vertically with a piece of the root in each slice.
4. Rotate vegetable on its axis for the next slice. Each slice will be like a small wedge. Slices may be thick or thin.

Note: Any round vegetable can be cut in crescents.

Flowers

1. Cut vegetable into 3- or 4-inch sections.
2. Make 3 or 4 V-cuts along the length of the vegetable.
3. Slice across.

Note: Pieces can be thin or thick.

Rounds

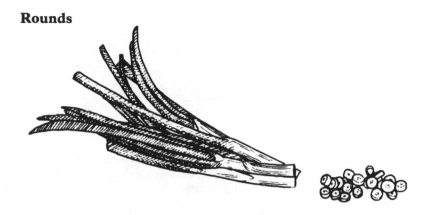

Slice across vegetable, thin or thick as desired.

Half and quarter rounds

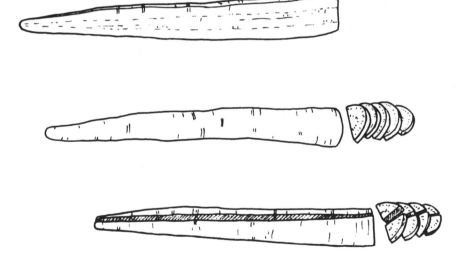

1. Slice vegetable in half lengthwise. For quarter rounds, slice each piece lengthwise in half again.
2. Place cut side down.
3. Slice across.
Note: Pieces can be thin or thick.

Diagonals

Slice diagonally across the vegetable, adjusting the length of the diagonal by the angle of the cut, and making thin or thick pieces as desired. Hold the knife perpendicular to the board.

Chunks

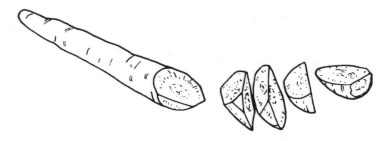

1. Place vegetable with stem end closest to knife.
2. Cut a thick diagonal cut.
3. Roll vegetable 90 degrees towards you.
4. Cut another thick diagonal.
5. Roll again and cut. Pieces will have 3 to 4 cut edges.
Note: Make long diagonals farther apart for larger chunks.

Matchsticks

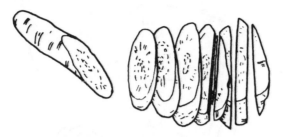

1. Slice vegetable into diagonals.
2. Overlap diagonal slices, if they haven't fallen into position when cut.
3. Slice diagonals lengthwise into matchsticks.
Note: Pieces can be thick or thin, as desired. Pieces can also be long or short, depending on the length of the diagonals. Each diagonal can be cut individually, but it takes longer than when pieces overlap.

Shaved

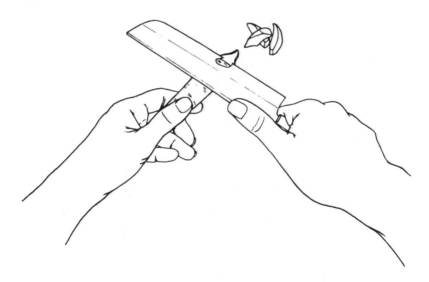

1. Hold vegetable in your hand straight away from your body.
2. Shave the vegetable by cutting away from the body as if sharpening a pencil or whittling.
Note: Shavings can be long or thick as desired.

Logs or paper cut

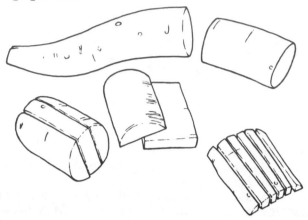

1. Slice vegetable across into 2 to 3-inch long sections.
2. Slice each section into vertical slabs.
3. Slice each slab into vertical rectangles.
Note: Very thin rectangles look more like sheets of paper while thick
   rectangles look more like logs.

Diced or minced

1. Slice vegetable lengthwise into vertical slabs.
2. Slice each slab into vertical logs.
3. Slice across the logs, thin or thick as desired.
Note: This dice cut can be varied to make cubes or thin squares. Minced
   pieces are very small. This cut can be used on round or long root
   vegetables.

Cubes

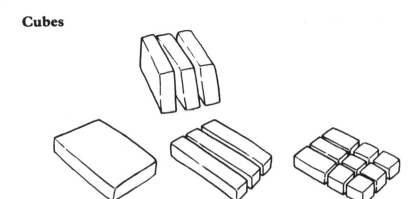

1. Cut tofu into slabs.
2. Cut each slab into logs.
3. Cut each log (or set of logs) into cubes.
Note: Cubes can be large or small.

Squares, squash

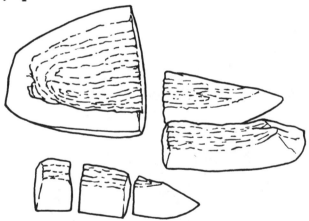

1. Cut stem from squash.
2. Slice squash lengthwise.
3. Remove seeds with a metal spoon.
4. Slice one half into lengthwise pieces.
5. Slice lengthwise pieces into squares.
Note: One side of each square will have skin. Squares can be large or
    small.

Squares, greens

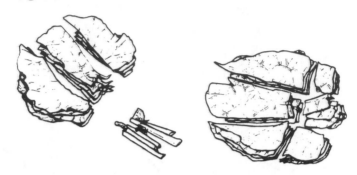

1. Place greens flat on top of each other. Notice where the leaf and stem meet. All these junctions should be on top of each other. This causes the bottoms of the stems to be uneven with each other, but will make the greens easier to cut.
2. Cut the stems as desired (rounds are often used).
3. Slice leaves into lengthwise pieces.
4. Slice across the pieces into squares.

Note: Squares can be large or small.

Shredded

1. Cut cabbage into 4 wedges (crescent cut).
2. Remove core.
3. Place one wedge with a cut side down.
4. Slice thinly across leaves.

Note: Shred is a fine cut. Cut fine or very fine. To shred leafy greens, follow steps 1 and 2 for squares, above, then cut thinly across the leaves.

Cored

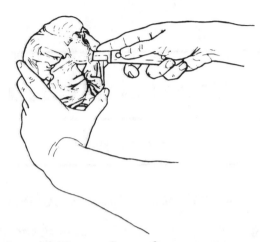

1. Hold the whole vegetable on a flat surface, core up.
2. Cut all around core with a strong paring knife, angling knife toward the center of the cabbage.
3. Remove core by lifting out. It will be pointed.

Flowerettes

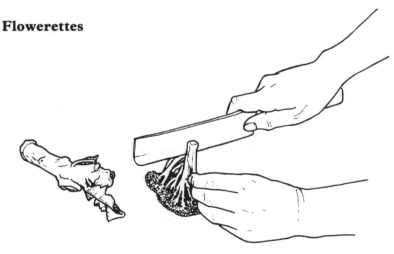

1. Cut broccoli below the flower at whatever length is desired.
2. Hold the flower on the board with the stem pointing up.
3. Cut into the stem toward the flower, but cut only the stem.
4. Divide the flower by pulling gently with your fingers.
Note: For cauliflower, remove the hard bottom stem. Place stem side up and divide by cutting into the stem, as above.

Suggested Readings

Cookbooks

Aihara, Cornellia – *The Calendar Cookbook,* GOMF, Oroville, 1979.

Aihara, Cornellia – *The Dō of Cooking,* GOMF, Oroville, 1982. Originally published as a four-volume set in 1971.

Aihara, Cornellia – *Macrobiotic Kitchen,* Japan Publications, Tokyo, 1984. Formerly published by GOMF as *The Chico-san Cookbook* in 1972.

Albright, Nancy – *The Rodale Cookbook,* Rodale, Emmaus, 1973.

Belleme, Jan and John – *Cooking with Japanese Foods,* East West, Brookline, 1986.

Colbin, Annemarie – *The Book of Whole Meals,* Ballantine, New York, 1979.

East West Journal – *The Whole World Cookbook,* Avery, Wayne, 1982.

Esko, Edward and Wendy – *Macrobiotic Cooking for Everyone,* Japan Publications, Tokyo, 1980.

Esko, Wendy – *Introducing Macrobiotic Cooking,* Japan Publications, Tokyo, 1978.

Estella, Mary – *Natural Foods Cookbook,* Japan Publications, Tokyo, 1985.

Ford, Marjorie, Susan Hillyard, and Faulk Koock – *Deaf Smith Country Cookbook,* Collier, New York, 1973.

George Ohsawa Macrobiotic Foundation – *The First Macrobiotic Cookbook*, GOMF, Oroville, 1985. Originally published as *Zen Cookery* by the Ohsawa Foundation of Los Angeles in 1964.

Kushi, Aveline – *Complete Guide to Macrobiotic Cooking*, Warner, New York, 1985.

Kushi, Aveline – *How to Cook with Miso*, Japan Publications, New York, 1978.

Kushi, Aveline, and Wendy Esko – *Changing Seasons Macrobiotic Cookbook*, Avery, Wayne, 1985.

Lappe, Frances Moore – *Diet for a Small Planet*, Ballantine, New York, 1971.

McCarty, Meredith – *American Macrobiotic Cuisine*, Turning Point, Eureka, 1986.

Ohsawa, Lima – *Macrobiotic Cuisine*, Japan Publications, Tokyo, 1984. Formerly published as *The Art of Just Cooking* by Autumn Press in 1974.

Robertson, Laurel, Carol Flinders, and Bronwen Godfrey – *Laurel's Kitchen*, Nilgiri, Berkeley, 1976.

Rombauer, Irma S., and Marion Rombauer Becker – *The Joy of Cooking*, Bobbs-Merrill, New York, 1964.

Shurtleff, William and Akiko Aoyagi – *The Book of Tofu*, 1975 and *The Book of Miso*, 1976, Ballantine, New York.

Weber, Marcea – *The Sweet Life*, Japan Publications, Tokyo, 1981.

Using Other Cookbooks

In general – You don't need to throw out all your favorite cookbooks if you wish to cook macrobiotically. In fact, it is much better to use and adapt them to fit your needs. Here are tips for using vegetarian, ethnic, or traditional cookbooks.

Compatible recipes – Look for a feasible recipe, one you can use without having to change the most important ingredients. For example, changing a recipe for pot roast and potatoes to one of brown rice and carrots is not reasonable. Changing a recipe for pizza with canned foods to one with fresh cooked foods is possible.

Interpreting recipes: easy or difficult – Read through the recipe to see what is generally done. How much skill is required? How many steps are involved? How many utensils are used? A recipe with many steps and utensils is harder and more time consuming than a recipe with few steps and utensils. Skills such as rolling out dough, crimping edges together, and frosting a cake can be difficult if you are trying them for the first time.

Adapting recipes – Change the recipe by substituting good quality alternatives for foods not desired. Use oil instead of butter, whole grain pasta for white pasta, arrowroot powder for cornstarch. When a recipe requires sugar, milk, or meat, it is harder to adapt.

Change recipes by combining or adding procedures. If the recipe calls for steaming the vegetables and then mixing with butter, change it to one step of sauteing the vegetables in oil. If the recipe calls for a blended raw tofu dip, change it and boil the tofu before blending.

When changing recipes, remember to keep the same consistency to create a similar end product. Check the ratios of the original recipe. Is it moist? Salty? Oily? Make the altered recipe similar.

Balance – Check recipe for balance considerations to see if it calls for many extreme yin items or yang items. If a recipe calls for ginger juice and sake over mushrooms without any salt, change it and add a salt (perhaps soy sauce) for a better balance. If a cooked fruit recipe has no salt, cook with a pinch of salt. If a fish recipe has salt or soy sauce without any yin quality, add a yin factor such as ginger. This step may be the one which determines the success or failure of the recipe.

Macrobiotic Thought

Aihara, Herman – *Acid and Alkaline,* 5th edition, GOMF, Oroville, 1986.

Aihara, Herman – *Basic Macrobiotics,* Japan Publications, Tokyo, 1985.

Aihara, Herman – *Kaleidoscope: Macrobiotic Articles, Essays, and Lectures, 1979-1985,* GOMF, Oroville, 1986.

Aihara, Herman – *Learning from Salmon,* GOMF, Oroville, 1980.

Colbin, Annemarie – *Food and Healing,* Ballantine, New York, 1986

Kushi, Michio – *The Book of Macrobiotics,* Japan Publications, Tokyo, 1977.

Kushi, Michio and Aveline – *Macrobiotic Diet,* Japan Publications, Tokyo, 1985.

Kushi, Michio – *The Macrobiotic Way,* Avery, Wayne, 1985.

Kushi, Michio – *Natural Healing through Macrobiotics,* Japan Publications, Tokyo, 1978.

Miller, Saul and JoAnne – *Food for Thought,* Prentice Hall, Englewood Cliffs, 1979.

Muramoto, Noboru – *Healing Ourselves,* Avon, New York, 1973.

Ohsawa, George – *The Book of Judgment,* GOMF, Oroville, 1980.

Ohsawa, George – *Macrobiotics: An Invitation to Health and Happiness,* GOMF, Oroville, 1971.

Ohsawa, George – *Macrobiotics: The Way of Healing,* GOMF, Oroville, 1984. Formerly published as *Cancer and the Philosophy of the Far East* by Swan House in 1971.

Ohsawa, George – *The Order of the Universe,* GOMF, Oroville, 1986.

Ohsawa, George – *Zen Macrobiotics,* Ohsawa Foundation, Los Angeles, 1965.

Sattilaro, Anthony, M.D. – *Living Well Naturally,* Houghton Mifflin, Boston, 1984.

A Word on Supplies and Suppliers

Many stores are beginning to carry more and more of the foods and supplies needed for following a macrobiotic diet. There are several mail order companies and larger distributors at present. The publisher of this book maintains a current list of suppliers and a complete catalog of macrobiotic books. Contact them at 1511 Robinson Street, Oroville, California 95965, (916) 533-7702 for the most recent information.

Index

Other books from the
George Ohsawa Macrobiotic Foundation

Acid and Alkaline - Herman Aihara; 1986; 121 pp; $8.95

Art of Peace - George Ohsawa; 1990; 150 pp; $7.95

As Easy As 1, 2, 3 - Pamela Henkel and Lee Koch; 1990; 176 pp; $6.95

Cooking with Rachel - Rachel Albert; 1989; 328 pp; $12.95

Essential Ohsawa - George Ohsawa, edited by Carl Ferré; 1994; 238 pp; $12.95

First Macrobiotic Cookbook - G.O.M.F.; 1985; 140 pp; $9.95

Gandhi, the Eternal Youth - George Ohsawa; 1986; 140 pp; $6.95

Kaleidoscope - Herman Aihara; 1986; 338 pp; $12.95

Macrobiotic Guidebook for Living - George Ohsawa; 1985; 130 pp; $7.95

Macrobiotics: An Invitation to Health and Happiness - George Ohsawa; 1971; 128 pp; $5.95

Macrobiotics: The Way of Healing - George Ohsawa; 1981; 165 pp; $8.95

Natural Healing from Head to Toe - Cornellia and Herman Aihara with Carl Ferré; 1994; 264 pp; $14.95

Naturally Healthy Gourmet - Margaret Lawson with Tom Monte; 1994; 232 pp; $14.95

Order of the Universe - George Ohsawa; 1986; 103 pp; $7.95

Philosophy of Oriental Medicine - George Ohsawa; 1991; 153 pp; $10.95

Pocket Guide to Macrobiotics - Carl Ferré; 1997; 128 pp; $6.95

Zen Macrobiotics, Unabridged Edition - George Ohsawa, edited by Carl Ferré; 1995; 206 pp; $9.95

A complete selection of macrobiotic books is available from the George Ohsawa Macrobiotic Foundation, P.O. Box 426, Oroville, California 95965; (916) 533-7702. Order toll free: **(800) 232-2372.**